Christian Martial Arts 101

Wendy Williamson

Christian Martial Arts 101

International Standard Book Number: 0-9721328-1-3

Library of Congress Catalog Card Number: 2004091490

Agapy Publishing
Kalamazoo, MI
Website: http://www.agapy.com
Email: info@agapy.com

Printed in the United States of America

First printing, October, 2004

Table of Contents

Dedication

Dear Leonardo,

This book is dedicated to you, my beautiful son. May God raise you up in His love, fruit, and power, into a mighty disciple and soldier of the Lord Jesus Christ. May you walk with Him always and forever, in His eternal life.

I love you so much. You bring a great joy to my life that I never knew before. Blessings to you always.

Love,
Your Mama

Acknowledgements

First and foremost, I'd like to sincerely thank my Lord and Savior, Jesus Christ, for giving me life, talent, and ability to write about Him and His love for the world. If it weren't for Jesus, this book would have never been possible.

Special thanks to my husband, Francisco, who supports me and helps me accomplish all of the goals that the Lord places in my heart. I really love you, Sweetie. God bless you always.

About the Author

Ms. Wendy is a Christian martial arts instructor and holds an MA degree in Counselor Education. She has been training in the martial arts for over twenty years and has taught Christ-centered karate classes around the world (in the United States, Africa, and South America), in three different languages. Ms. Wendy is Founder and Director of the Christian Martial Arts Program at Agape Christian Church (Kalamazoo, MI) and a member of various Christian martial arts associations that strive to reach people with the Gospel. She is also the author of the well-known book, *Martial Arts: The Christian Way*.

How to Use this Book

Christian Martial Arts 101 is intended for Christian martial artists and any Christ-centered martial arts program in need of a spiritual curriculum to complement physical training. This book can also be used as a personal devotional for Christian students attending non-religious martial arts schools. It establishes and explains the major principles of Christian martial arts and includes 101 Bible lessons/devotions for use in the classroom and at home.

In terms of doctrine, *Christian Martial Arts 101* establishes Jesus Christ as Master and the Bible as the Code for training. It contains 101 Bible lessons divided into nine of thirteen chapters. Each lesson ends with a principle and two or more codes. The principle sums up the teachings. The codes are the scripture sources for the teachings and should be looked up in the Bible after reading the lesson. *Christian Martial Arts 101* is written from a charismatic perspective and assumes that the reader accepts that Jesus is Lord of all.

Finally, this book comes in two separate editions: a regular edition (ISBN 0-9721328-1-3) and an instructor's edition (ISBN 0-9721328-2-1). The regular edition is written for Christian martial artists who are over ten years of age. The instructor's edition is identical to the regular edition, but includes added resources that instructors can use in designing a class format/curriculum and developing Bible lessons for children under the age of ten.

Table of Lessons

Warning—Disclaimer

Chapter 1

Excuse me, Christian Martial Arts? (ha ha)

For the foolishness of God
is wiser than man's wisdom
and the weakness of God
is stronger than man's strength.

~ 1 Corinthians 1:25, NIV

If you are or have ever been a Christian and a martial artist at the same time, then you've probably heard criticism from family members, friends, or complete strangers sometime during your life. Most likely, this criticism caused you to do at least one of three things: (1) quit the martial arts entirely, (2) redefine yourself as a Christian, and/or (3) learn how to defend yourself and your Lord from critical attacks. Whichever way you responded in the past, you must see some correlation between Christianity and martial arts; otherwise you wouldn't be reading this book.

I kid you not when I say that this book is going to blow your socks off; it totally and completely redefines martial arts with a Christian worldview. It doesn't subscribe to any particular style or form and can be used to teach and preach the Gospel through any Christ-centered program or school. Contrary to popular belief, God made martial arts. He is now reclaiming them to do His will in this world and bring His message to the ends of the earth. Whatever martial arts were, whatever you thought they were, and whatever you wanted them to be is entirely irrelevant unless it lines up with God's purpose. Everything and everyone in heaven and on earth belong to God (Ps. 24 1-2; Col. 1:16-17).

If we really believe that all on earth belongs to God, then we will treat everything and everyone on earth as such. Satan loves to steal from God and he does so by getting us to listen to and believe his lies. A prime example is the proliferation of criminal and immoral activity in the United States. Satan has taken good gifts from God (such as financial prosperity and sexual intimacy) and made them into cheap traps to be used for selfish gain and personal pleasure. Sadly enough, many have fallen victim to Satan's lies and have cast their pearls before swine (Matt. 7:6).

Martial arts are another example of a gift given to us by God that Satan has tried to steal. Martial arts knowledge, skills, and abilities originally came from God; however, they were misused by man and made into cheap traps by Satan for personal pleasure and selfish gain. As Christians, we must learn how to reclaim the things that Satan steals from God and use them as He intended, for His glory. We must learn to battle against the lies and deception that Satan spreads to get people to disregard God's creation.

Through Bible study, meditation, and prayer, God has taught me how to reclaim Christian martial arts for His Glory. He has also taught me how to answer questions and educate other people about Christian martial arts. Below is a synopsis of what the Lord has taught me. This is how I present Christian martial arts to the public and how I distinguish them as a collective tool that can be used for God's glory and honor, to raise up mighty men and women under the Lord Jesus Christ.

How can Christians be involved in martial arts?

There are two ways that Christians can Biblically be involved in the martial arts:

1. By completely removing Eastern religious concepts that may be attached and doing physical techniques as a form of exercise or sport. There is nothing wrong with martial arts. You reap the health benefits from training as you would in any other sport; in addition,

you learn how to protect and defend yourself and others under various circumstances.

2. By replacing Eastern religious concepts with Christian ones. In this way, the martial arts become a tool for growth and development in the Christian faith and life, in addition to an exercise or sport. Clearly, there are physical, mental, and spiritual health benefits for those who train in this way.

While this book supports and condones both approaches, it's primarily written for those who use martial arts in the second way, to reach out to people with the Gospel and help them come to know Christ and grow in their faith.

Tell me more about the second way. How does a Christian way of life fit with martial arts?

There are many ways that martial arts lend themselves to Christian teaching. I have identified seven major ways and an infinite number of minor ways that can help people make the connection.

1. THROUGH THE CONCEPT OF MASTER

Martial arts are traditionally taught with the concept of Master, either as an instructor or as a figure in the background. In Christian martial arts, the Master is Christ and the teachings are His, from the Bible. "And don't let anyone call you 'Master,' for there is only one master, the Messiah" (Matt. 23:10, NLT). Christian black belts, no matter what degree, are not masters of anything; they are disciples of the Lord Jesus Christ.

2. THROUGH THE CONCEPT OF WARFARE

Martial arts means *fighting arts*. While plain old martial arts train only the physical and the mental self in the art of war, Christian martial arts train the spiritual, too. The Bible tells us that we do not fight against flesh and blood, but against evil rulers and authorities, against mighty powers of darkness that rule in an unseen world. Ephesians 6:11-18 is very clear that as Christians, we are mighty soldiers on God's side of the battlefield. Surely, we need to learn how to fight.

3. THROUGH BIBLICAL STRATEGIES IN PROTECTION AGAINST EVIL

People learn the martial arts to protect and defend themselves and others from evil. Christians use the Word of God and the techniques of martial arts to protect and defend themselves and others from evil and sin that comes from the tricks and strategies of the devil. Christian martial artists believe that the root of evil in the world is the devil, since he influences and takes captive people that God made and designed. God said, "For every living soul belongs to me" (Ezek. 18:4, NIV). Christ offers a second chance to everyone, all sinners, including those who have done the most detestable things.

4. THROUGH THE CONCEPT OF TOTAL-PERSON TRAINING

Traditionally, martial arts have been about total person training (body, mind, and spirit). The Bible also teaches us that we are to love God with our total person (Matt. 22:37, Mark 12:30, Luke 10:27). Christian martial arts help students learn how to love God with all their heart, mind, soul, and strength (mentally and physically). They do a good job of bringing the body back into spiritual discipline as a temple for Jesus Christ to live and work, in an age when people are so readily defiling their bodies with junk food, laziness, sexual immorality, etc.

5. THROUGH SPECTACULAR YOUTH APPEAL

Traditionally, martial arts have attracted a large number of youth. The mere attraction combined with the mental, physical, and spiritual teachings sets them up to be powerful ministry/outreach tools for Christians. The Bible tells us to find common ground with others so that we can bring them to Christ (1 Cor. 9:19-23).

6. THROUGH UNIQUE TEACHING STYLES

While lectures and sermons are good, martial arts offer a very different form of Christian education that involves the total person in the learning process, including the body. This deepens learning and is especially well-suited for the energy levels of youths. It's our job to find creative ways of getting people to not only listen to the Word, but to do what it says physically, mentally, and spiritually (Jas. 1:22).

7. THROUGH GOAL-DRIVEN RANKS

Martial arts have traditionally been developmental and goal-oriented, steering students to a path of personal development from white to black belt and teaching them how to set and reach goals. Christianity is also developmental and goal-oriented. Paul clearly outlined the importance of setting and reaching goals in 1 Corinthians 9:24-27.

Why are some Christians against martial arts?

Some Christians do not understand martial arts because in mainstream society they are often associated with myst-icism, violence, and warfare, as well as Eastern culture, religion, and philosophy. Christians may also misinterpret or misread scripture from the Bible or take it out of context.

What are some of the things you hear from those who think martial arts are anti-Christian and how do you respond?

1. *Christianity and martial arts are contradictory.*

Any attempt to prove that martial arts are compatible or incompatible with Christianity is a moot point. The martial arts as a collective whole is not a religion, and cannot logically be compared to one. Grapefruits and oranges are comparable because they are both fruits, but baskets and apples are not comparable in the human scheme of logic.

On the other hand, martial arts are a lot like a basket. Just as a basket is capable of holding any fruit; martial arts are capable of holding the beliefs of any religion. Much like rock music can be used to minister to youth and glorify God by changing the lyrics and focus to Christ, so can the martial arts.

2. *Self-defense is unbiblical; Jesus said turn the other cheek.*

My first response is: what would you do if you were walking down the street at night and saw someone being beaten up...if you found a so-called friend sexually abusing your five-year-old daughter...if a crazed lunatic broke into your house in an attempt to steal and harm? Would you allow it all to happen?

The teaching in the *Turn the Other Cheek* parable (Matt. 5:39) is not about protecting lives; it's about responding to insult. It's not a major threat to anyone's physical or emotional well-being to get slapped across the face or insulted. The Bible teaches us that when we are insulted, we should not react out of anger, rather we should respond out of love.

Our responses are teachable moments; it's during these moments when people make judgments about who we are compared to whom we profess to be. If someone insults me and I haul off and punch him, then I'm not using the moment to demonstrate God's love; I'm not being self-controlled as the Holy Bible advocates, and I'm not giving Christians a very good reputation either.

In 1 Corinthians 13:7, the Bible tells us that Love protects (NIV) and beareth (KJV). The original Greek word used in the New Testament is "stego." Stego means to keep or protect by covering, to shield from something that threatens. The Bible also tells us that the greatest commandment is to love God and our neighbors as ourselves. So, in essence, the Bible commands us to protect God, our neighbors, and ourselves from threats and harm's way. If we find ourselves witnessing ungodliness, we are called to step up and protect God, His Name, and His Son.

3. *The Bible is about peace and love, not war.*

The Bible is full of vigilance, battles, and wars led by great men of God. David wrote, "Blessed be the LORD my strength, which teacheth my hands to war, and my fingers to fight" (Ps. 144:1 KJV). When common laborers were rebuilding the walls of Jerusalem, they worked with one hand and held a weapon with the other; all the builders had swords attached to their belts (Neh. 4:17-18). God Himself approved battle. "When you go out to fight your enemies and you face horses and chariots and an army greater than your own, do not be afraid. The LORD your God, who brought you safely out of Egypt, is with you" (Deut. 20:1 NLT).

In fact, God told Israel to destroy everyone who was

in the land that they would possess. "As for the towns of the nations the LORD your God is giving you as a special possession, destroy every living thing in them. You must completely destroy the Hittites, Amorites, Canaanites, Perizzites, Hivites, and Jebusites, just as the LORD your God has commanded you. This will keep the people of the land from teaching you their detestable customs in the worship of their gods, which would cause you to sin deeply against the LORD your God" (Deut. 20:16-18 NLT).

4. *Martial arts are violent; they teach people how to kick butt.*

Even in secular martial arts schools, students are taught that it's better to avoid a single conflict than to win 1000 battles. Valor in the martial arts is the ability to remain self-controlled during intense and heated moments. Compared to football or hockey, the martial arts are like ballet, mainly because they are an art as much as they are a sport. In fact, martial arts actually teach students how to *turn the other cheek*, and respond to insult in a Godly way.

Trained martial artists know that responding to insult in a gentle way softens our enemies' hearts and puts us in a valorous and advantageous position. Romans 12:19-21 demonstrates the wisdom of responding gently rather than reacting out of hurt feelings or furiously heated moments; "Dearly beloved, avenge not yourselves, but rather give place unto wrath: for it is written, Vengeance is mine; I will repay, saith the Lord. Therefore if thine enemy hunger, feed him; if he thirst, give him drink: for in so doing thou shalt heap coals of fire on his head. Be not overcome of evil, but overcome evil with good" (Rom. 12:19-21 KJV).

Psychologists say the same thing. If someone raises her voice out of anger, our natural response is to raise our voice, too; this just escalates and intensifies the argument. However, if we make a conscious effort to soften our voice, even though we feel very angry, the argument will die down to a friendly discussion. Our responses often fuel the reactions of others. When we are aware of this and learn to control our emotions, we find ourselves arguing less and communicating more.

5. *Fighting is unbiblical. Jesus told his own disciple to put away his sword.*

Matthew 26:50-54 is another set of scriptures that skeptics often like to quote to prove that fighting is unbiblical; however, when taken in context, these verses actually support fighting. In these verses, Judas came with a multitude to take Jesus to Caiaphas, the high priest. When they tried to seize Jesus, Peter sliced off the ear of a servant of the high priest with his sword and prepared to engage in a fight. Jesus stopped him and told him to put away his sword. He did so because He knew a fight in this situation would be in opposition to His very purpose; Jesus knew it was a part of God's plan that He surrender to the multitude, die on the cross, and be resurrected. Jesus was not opposed to fighting; in fact, He ordered the disciples to sell their clothes and buy a sword if they didn't already have one (Luke 22:36-38). After all, it was God who invented the sword and the fight, to bring glory and honor to Him.

6. *One of the Ten Commandments is DO NOT KILL.*

Actually, Exodus 20:13 commands us not to murder. Murder is premeditated and the term was never used in the Bible when referring to self-defense. Exodus 22:2-3 tells us if a thief is killed in the act of breaking into a house, then so be it; it's self-defense and the killer is not guilty of anything at all. However, if a thief is killed in the daylight, after the break-in is over, then the killer is guilty of murder in the eyes of God. In other words, if we end up killing someone in a legitimate defense, it's understandable, but if we kill out of a revengeful heart after a wrongful act was committed, then it's not excusable and is considered to be murder. As you can see, there is a difference between killing and murdering.

Chapter 2

The Making of a
Christian Martial Artist

Therefore, since we are surrounded
by such a huge crowd of witnesses
to the life of faith, let us strip off
every weight that slows us down,
especially the sin that so easily
hinders our progress.
And let us run with endurance
the race that God has set before us.

~ Hebrews 12:1, NLT

Christians are weak, right? Wrong! Christians are not weak; they are the strongest and most capable group of people on earth! While they are not necessarily the strongest physically, they are invested with a strength of character and purpose that has significance in this life and the one to come. God is the all-powerful creator of everything we know, and Christians are His people. As stated in Hebrews 12:1, Christians run a race that God has set before them. They do not walk and they do not jog; they run, and they run to win! Through endurance and perseverance, God prepares them to do His will and fulfills His purpose in their lives.

Regardless of whether or not you were raised in a Christian home, you probably came to a point in your life where you personally accepted your salvation through Jesus Christ and formed an intimate relationship with God. If not, then hopefully you will by the end of this book. Christianity is not about following rules and being regulated by a higher power, it's about a relationship—a Father uniting Himself with us through His Son, who became one of us and died for us. It's about a decision we make with our own freewill that allows Him to come into our lives and be what He created us to be.

When we make a decision to accept Jesus in our lives, we enter into Christ's death and resurrection, dying to our old lives and our slavery to sin. We become newborn babies in the Christian faith. Everything is new and exciting. As we read the Bible, we begin to drink the milk of the Word and grow. We learn how to roll over, sit up, crawl, and eventually walk, jump, punch, and kick with God through faith. We learn how to listen to His Spirit speak to us through His Word, to reach out to God and talk to Him through prayer, to play with Him, and work with Him. He becomes our resting place, as we live our lives in Him daily.

We realize that our salvation, our relationship with God, is about loving Him and allowing Him to love us. Much like children go through phases with their parents, we go through phases with God. At first we are totally infatuated with Him and excited to be one of His children. As we get a little older (in the Lord), we hit our "terrible two's," and we think that God isn't meeting our wants and needs like He promised in His Word. Just as mommy says "no" to her three-year old child when he wants to touch a hot stove, God says "no" to us when we want to do something that He knows will hurt us. We don't understand, so we throw a tantrum and run.

God also allows things to happen that we don't like. It could be someone close to us passes away or that we are stricken with illness, poverty, or misfortune. Remember, God is our parent and He knows what is best for us. His purpose for someone else may be with Him in Heaven and His purpose for you may be that you learn how to lose what you love and release it to Him. If you are one of His children, you may get hurt, but rest assured that He will turn everything around in your life for good. If you are not one of His children, well, you'll still get hurt, but won't have His turn-around effect.

Eventually, we come into a more mature, steady relationship. As His Word so elegantly speaks, we learn how to love God with our heart, mind, soul, and strength (Mark 12:30). We realize that it's difficult to do what God tells us to do all the time, but that we must learn the value of discipline in doing it anyway. We read and study God's Word and try to make sense of things that He tells us to do in a world full of pain and suffering. The Holy Spirit begins to work full-time in our lives to make us like Christ. We learn to love our neighbors the way in which we love ourselves, and the Fruit of the Spirit grows fervently in our lives as a beautiful expression of God's love.

As we mature in our love and faith in the Lord, we learn to wear and use the Armor of God, too. We become skilled in the use of His helmet, His shield, His sword, His shoes, and His belt. We use this armor not only to protect ourselves from the snares and traps of the devil, but to protect others as well. We cannot see the spiritual battlefield in this world full of pain and suffering, but we live right in the middle of it. By training with the armor, strength and power that comes from God, we become fit and equipped to nurture and protect our souls in life, so that they can enjoy an eternal afterlife with their Creator.

Finally, we are grownup Christians, ready to go out into the world, and fulfill the Great Commission by bringing souls to the Lord Jesus Christ. We have entered into the third season of life and have begun to work in a professional capacity for the Lord. We become soldiers in God's army of teachers and evangelists. We go into battlefields (be it our neighborhoods, our schools, our jobs), and fight off the misconceptions and lies about God. We help to give birth to babes in the Lord, to feed them spiritual milk, to be with them when they learn how to walk and talk, to teach them how to work and play, and to raise them up into mighty men and women.

As grownups in the Lord, we continue to grow, by taking two steps forward and one step back, and by allowing God to carry us when we just can't seem to make it on our own. That's what being a Christian is all about, realizing that we can't and aren't intended to go it alone, we need Jesus Christ living through our lives as Savior and Lord. Without Jesus Christ in our lives, we are wretched and filthy (Mark 7:21-23); our bones waste away and we moan and groan out of pure misery (Ps. 32:1-5). Without Jesus Christ, we are weak and susceptible to failure. We cannot punch, kick, stand, jump, break boards, perform kata, or do anything else in martial arts either.

So, what does all this have to do with Christian martial arts? Well, everything! There is a difference between a Christian who practices martial arts and a Christian martial artist. Being Christian and driving a car doesn't make you a Christian car driver. Being a Christian and eating a burger doesn't make you a Christian burger eater, either. So how does being a Christian and practicing martial arts make you a Christian martial artist? It doesn't! You can be a martial artist and a Christian, but it really does take a lot more to be a Christian martial artist.

If you don't want to mix Christianity and martial arts, fine. It's between you and God. Let me just ask you one question though…what's your ultimate purpose for living? After all, no matter how hard you train, it isn't going last forever. A Christian martial artist is one who uses the martial arts as a tool to live out his/her life in the Lord Jesus Christ and to help other people come to know Jesus Christ and live their lives for Him, too. This lines up with the Word, which tells us that anything and everything Christians do must be for the glory of God (1 Cor. 10:31). Consequently, as Christian martial artists we are always training on the road to:

- Eternal salvation through Jesus Christ
- A Personal relationship with God
- Loving God with our heart, soul, mind, and strength
- Loving our neighbors as ourselves
- Character development through the Fruit of the Spirit
- Spiritual warfare with the full Armor of God
- Evangelism and the Great Commission

Christian martial artists are committed to developing a set of ideals in their lives. They are loyal to these ideals in the same way that the Samurai were loyal to the Code of Bushido and the Medieval Knights were loyal to the Code of Chivalry. The ideals that shape the lives of Christian martial artists don't come from different traditions and styles. They don't come from taekwondo, karate, yoga, or tai chi. The ideals come from one book, known as *The Bible*, and they form one Code, known as *The Christian Way*. The principles are as follows:

Salvation and Eternal Life (Chapter 5)
Christian martial artists accept their Salvation through the Son of God, which results in eternal life. Because of sin, people were separated and cut off from God; the only way back to Him and eternal life is through Christ, Son of God. Jesus Christ is the only truth, way, and life (John 14:6).

Physical–Mental–Spiritual Relationship (Chapter 6)
Christian martial artists love God with their bodies, minds, and souls. As a soldier prepares physically, mentally, and spiritually to protect a nation, her freedoms and beliefs, a Christian martial artist prepares physically, mentally, and spiritually to love God and do His will on earth.

Loving My Neighbors as Myself (Chapter 7)
Christian martial artists love their neighbors as themselves. While the focus is on our neighbors, it's important to realize that we cannot love our neighbors if we do not love ourselves (body, mind, and soul). When we love ourselves, we are whole; when we do not love ourselves, we are dysfunctional, unable to love others as God intended.

The Fruit of the Spirit (Chapter 8)
Christian martial artists produce the Fruit of the Spirit. The Fruit of the Spirit is God's expression of intimacy and love in our lives and relationships. When the Holy Spirit is flowing freely within us, we naturally produce Fruit, expressing His very nature. When the Holy Spirit is blocked because of selfish ambition, God's expression of intimacy and love is prevented from flowing in and through our lives.

The Full Armor of God (Chapter 9)
Christian martial artists put on the full armor of God. The Full Armor of God is God's protection over our lives when we are dealing with temptation, the devil, and the evil forces of the world. Christian martial artists train to be militant soldiers in God's army, learning effective techniques, strategies, and tactics to overcome all things contrary to God and His ways.

The Great Warrior (Chapter 10)
Christian martial artists become great warriors. God calls us to protect others and ourselves from threat and harm. It's better to avoid a single conflict than to win 1000 battles; in other words, force is only allowed when absolutely crucial. Christian martial artists are committed to protect and defend the souls of all people by bringing them to Jesus Christ.

The Child of God (Chapter 11)
Christian martial artists should always remain childlike (not childish) in some ways. When we come into adulthood, new sets of responsibilities are inherited, but we do not cease to be God's children. Sometimes we forget. "I tell you the truth, unless you change and become like little children, you will never enter the kingdom of heaven" (Matt. 18:3, NIV).

The Great Commission (Chapter 12)
Christian martial artists are God's helpers. They go to all the corners of the earth and help Him bring the lost sheep home. "And he said unto them, Go ye into all the world, and preach the gospel to every creature. He that believeth and is baptized shall be saved; but he that believeth not shall be damned" (Mark 16:15-16, KJV).

The Christian Black Belt (Chapter 13)
Black belt is not the end of a walk; it's a new beginning. Christian black belts are equipped to bring all of the above ideals together and teach the Gospel through a Christian martial arts ministry. They are disciples of the Lord Jesus Christ and work for God by using their martial arts talents and every other gift that the Lord has bestowed on them.

Christian Martial Arts Pledge
Christian martial artists pledge allegiance to the cross of their Savior in much the same way that nationals pledge allegiance to the flag of their country and soldiers pledge allegiance to defend and protect their country. It's a great honor to be a Christian martial artist, but a great responsibility also.

If you are a Christian martial artist, this pledge is for you. Say it daily before your workouts and know who your master is in everything you are and do (JESUS is the MASTER!).

I pledge allegiance to the cross

of my Lord, Jesus Christ,

and to the love

for which it stands ...

one Savior, everlasting,

indivisible,

with mercy and grace

for all ~Amen

Chapter 3

THE HISTORY OF MARTIAL ARTS

And we know that God causes

everything to work together for

the good of those who love God

and are called according to His

purpose.

~ Romans 8:28, NLT

It's good to know where martial arts came from, but do not allow such information to limit your understanding of what martial arts are today. Every person and every culture has a past, full of human mistakes and blunders. Even the Bible is full of stories about people who really messed up, big time. Isn't that exactly why Christ had to come and save the world? Because God is so good and so awesome, He turned human mistakes and blunders into something purposeful: HISTORY. History is used in the Bible, and in the world, to teach us how to get things right, today. The purpose of history is to prevent future generations from repeating the mistakes of the past.

Unfortunately, the history of the martial arts was not well documented and we know very little about how it developed over thousands of years. Early Greek civilization practiced a martial art called *Pankration*, a mix of wrestling, grappling, throwing, and boxing techniques. Early Russian civilization developed a martial art called *Sambo*, which can be traced back to ancient times and is today taught to the Russian military as a form of hand-to-hand combat training. Early Roman culture developed fighting techniques with shields and weapons and entertained themselves with violent contests to the death between man and beast. Brazilian slaves created unique escapes, head butts, kicks, and sweeps, collectively known as *Capoeira*, to protect themselves from their masters.

While some forms of martial arts can be traced to nearly every continent, contemporary fighting systems owe their roots to East Asia: China, Japan, Okinawa, and Korea. East Asian governments permitted few freedoms before the nineteenth century, so people developed martial arts in secret to fight in regional combats and wars. These arts were covertly passed from earlier generations to the present.

China

In China, Shaolin monks developed the first unarmed and effective form of self-defense around the 5th Century. While it's unknown exactly when kung fu (also known as gung fu) came into existence, this style is known as the predecessor of all systematic Chinese martial arts. For many centuries, it was practiced and taught secretly and passed on from generation to generation among certain family clans.

In 1848, during the infamous Gold Rush, Chinese immigrants brought kung fu to the United States for the first time; even so, it was still taught and practiced in secrecy, only among Chinese families. It was not until 1964 that it was taught for the first time to outsiders. Shortly thereafter, in the 1970s, it became very popular as a result of television and film.Kung fu literally means "an acquired skill," in Cantonese. However, a more modern term for the collective study of Chinese martial arts is wu shu. There are various types of wu shu ranging from very hard styles like shaolin, to very soft styles like t'ai chi chuan.

The hard styles of wu shu focus on conditioning the body, developing physical power, and demonstrating strength. Examples include: wing chun, shaolin, kickboxing, kempo, t'ang lang, dragon, white crane, black crane, praying mantis, tiger, monkey, and snake. The soft styles focus on developing internal body functions (i.e. breathing and circulation) and demonstrating outward softness and fluidity. Examples include: t'ai chi, hsing-i, and pa kua.

The concept of chi is central to wu shu teaching and practice, especially in the soft styles. Unfortunately, many Christians mistake chi for sorcery and many non-Christian martial artists perpetuate this mistaken belief with outlandish claims about their powers. In truth, chi is nothing more than a developed awareness and focus of electro-chemical energy present in the body.

Everyone has heard stories about 100-pound women lifting up rear ends of automobiles to save loved ones in danger. That amazing stream of energy, which comes in the midst of desperation, is the most extreme form of chi. No one really understands how chi is activated to such an extreme, but it's real and has even been captured on film using Kirlian photography. While the concept of chi helps us push our minds and bodies to our own limits, nothing short of divine intervention helps us surpass those limits. The only creator of miracles is God.

While martial arts developed differently all over China, the differences are more apparent between the northern and southern parts of the country. The Northerners tended to kick about 70% of the time and punch about 30% of the time, and the Southerners tended toward just the opposite.

In the North, people had tall bodies and long arms and legs. Thus, their center of gravity was relatively high. They were naturally inclined to speed and focus because hunting and raising animals for survival was a part of their everyday lives. As martial artists, they were good with weapons, they had strong flying kicks, and they were more prone to practicing their arts through prearranged sequences than sparring.

In the South, people were short and small and their center of gravity was lower than that of the Northerners. They fished and cultivated crops, such as rice, on sizeable farms. As a result, their bodies developed a great deal of strength and endurance, which made them very powerful martial artists. They had strong-grounded techniques; they were skilled with their hands; and they were more prone to practicing their arts through sparring than prearranged sequences.

In spite of the differences between the northern and southern parts of China, there are more than 300 distinct styles, sub-styles, and family-based styles of Chinese martial arts. These styles emphasize different techniques, which may or may not include strikes, kicks, pressure points, weapons, grappling, throws, or ground fighting. They are all distinctly Chinese because of their rich history that began around 3500 BC. Thanks to Hollywood, wing chun (Bruce Lee's style) is probably one of the most popular styles of wu shu today.

Japan

In Japan, martial arts developed out of the samurai (Japanese warrior class) tradition of the 12th century. Samurai came from specific family clans; they received harsh training from childhood and they adhered to the Code of Bushido. The Code of Bushido was a code of ethics, similar to the knight's Code of Chivalry; it stood for unity, responsibility, and loyalty. The Code was so important to the samurai that they valued it above their own lives.

The function of the Japanese samurai was similar to the function of the medieval European knights, to protect and carry out the orders of their lords. The samurai had special privilege in society and the right to bear arms. However, if an enemy captured them, they were expected to take their own lives. It was dishonorable to be tortured or killed by an enemy; in such circumstances, suicide was the only honorable way out. Consequently, their superiors knew them as great servants, willing to die for the principles of a code, under responsibility and loyalty to their lords.

For more than five centuries, the samurai fought the tough feudal wars of Japan. They were the most prolific during the dictatorship of the Tokugawa era between 1600 and 1867. However, after the Meiji Restoration of 1868, the samurai began to decline. All loyalties to clan leaders were transferred to the royal leader of Japan, who initiated new legislation governing their continuation. Gradually, the samurai were stripped of their special privileges as a class and became ordinary citizens of the country. Japan's feudal battles ended, and finally after World War II, Japanese society started to emerge from its traditional ways to a more open society.

The samurai studied bujutsu (art of military combat) before the Meiji Restoration. From that point on, bushido evolved into budo (a modern-day military art) as the samurai knowledge began to be applied to life. Softer forms of the martial arts evolved, and the names of several martial arts styles were changed. Jujutsu was changed to judo, kenjutsu was changed to kendo, and aiki jutsu was changed to aikido. In essence, these name changes were made to reflect their new meanings; the "art" became the "way" of the martial disciplines, and the purpose shifted from combat to self-defense. Consequently, new sport-like traditions evolved.

Okinawa

In Okinawa, the martial arts originated in the Kingdom of Ryukyus. Part of its development was a direct result of the Japanese takeover from 1609 to 1945; during this period, the Japanese confiscated all weapons and left the Okinawans helpless to defend themselves. In retaliation, the Okinawans secretly learned and practiced karate, a mix of various arts from China, Japan, and India. It was not until the end of World War II that the Japanese surrendered and Okinawa became a recognized U.S. territory as well as a military base for American soldiers. After the war, many soldiers stayed in Okinawa and continued their schooling in karate.

Although Okinawa is essentially the birthplace of karate, Japan played a major role in polishing and dispersing it to the world. In 1917, and again in 1922, Gichin Funakoshi (a native Okinawan widely acknowledged as the founder of modern-day karate) was invited to Japan to perform a karate demonstration and introduce the art to a country that knew nothing about it. The Japanese clearly liked what they saw, enough to invite the Okinawan to stay in their country and teach the art.

In 1936, Funakoshi built his first karate school in Tokyo, and in 1948, he founded the Japan Karate Association. Even after his death in 1957, karate continued to flourish in Japan and eventually made its way around the globe. Some of today's most popular karate styles include shito-ryu, wado-ryu, goju-ryu, kyokushinkai, and shotokan. Many of these styles were brought to the United States by the Air Force between 1951 and 1966, when the Strategic Air Command sent its men to Japan for karate training, and have proliferated ever since.

Korea

In Korea, the martial arts trace back to the Shilla Dynasty, 668 to 935 AD, where there existed an elite group of young knights known as hwarang warriors. These warriors were physically and mentally trained in a type of hand-to-hand martial combat to prepare them for warfare. Much like the Japanese samurai, the hwarang were honorable, disciplined, and followed a strict moral code.

Subak, the first martial sports activity of Korea, developed during the Koryo Dynasty, from 935 to 1392 AD. This sport eventually evolved into hapkido and taekyon, which housed many martial arts schools. During the Koryo Dynasty, the state religion was Buddhism, which influenced the martial arts of the day. The Buddhists liked martial arts, so kings brought martial arts experts to the palace for various demonstrations. Consequently, martial arts became the royal sport of Korea.

In 1392, the Choson Dynasty (also called the Yi Dynasty) overturned the Koryo Dynasty; during this time, Buddhism collapsed and Confucianism took over as the state religion. Because physical force was looked down upon in Confucianism, martial arts quickly passed away and were banned in many regions of the country. Thus, committed martial artists were forced into secrecy. The Choson Dynasty lasted until 1909, when the Japanese took over.

From 1909 to 1945, Korea was under the control of Japan. During this period, the Japanese confiscated all weapons and left the people helpless to defend themselves against attacks.

While some continued to practice the martial arts underground, others fled to surrounding countries to continue their study. Those who fled Korea were exposed to the rise of karate in Japan and kung fu in China. By the time Korea was liberated at the end of World War II, they were masters in these other arts and returned to teach what they had learned.

It was not long before karate and kung fu, mixed with martial arts that developed out of Korea, evolved into several kwan schools (styles of Korean karate). In 1955, these kwan schools merged to form taekwondo, and in 1961, they formed the Korea Taekwondo Association. Only one of the kwan leaders decided that he couldn't come to an agreement with the others; thus, he formed a separate school and system called tang soo do. Another Korean martial arts style was systemized in 1963; this Korean form of aikido mixed with taekwondo and tang soo do is known today as hapkido.

Christian Martial Arts

The historical purpose of martial tradition was indeed to fight in combat and war. Martial artists trained for military combat were, as expected, callous, and destructive. However, with the advent of the modern mechanized military, martial arts in combat forces faded out (except for those in small, strategic strike forces like the Navy Seals). The purpose of the martial arts then became primarily for health and sport, and moral values and principles became a part of the tradition.

From that point on, the martial arts grew and evolved in different directions in accord with the cultures and religions of the various times and places. After the major wars of the 20th century (namely World War II and Vietnam), soldiers returned to the United States with martial arts skills. Coupled with the Charismatic Christian movement and the values of peace and love that dominated the 1960s, Christians started using the martial arts to teach spiritual lessons to people. Some used the spectacular tactics of the martial arts (like breaking boards and bricks) to grab attention and interject messages of Christianity and the Bible. Others formed their own Christian styles/systems of martial arts to influence students in Christianity on a day-to-day basis. Still others tied key concepts of the Bible to traditional styles.

In the 1990s, I taught Christian martial arts everywhere that I lived and worked, including third world countries I was sent to by the Peace Corps. I had no idea that so many martial artists around the world were doing the same thing until I returned to the United States and discovered the Worldwide Web. Before I left for the Peace Corps in 1994, the Internet was just a nice college-networking tool that I used for emailing my friends on campus, but after I returned, I found an international communication tool at my disposal...one that I had never fathomed before!

One day, I decided to do a keyword search on Christian Martial Arts and was amazed at the results. I found Christian schools, associations, homepages, and systems all over the Net. I thought it was fantastic, and it was, but after conferring with a variety of folks, I quickly learned (a) how little the Christian community knew about these arts, (b) how skeptical the public was about Christ-centered martial arts teachings, and (c) how much separation existed among the different Christian martial arts groups. For some reason, I felt burdened about the situation and prayed about it quite often.

In 2001, it occurred to me that God was putting a burden on my heart for a reason; He wanted me to use my gifts of writing to help people understand Christian martial arts and to bring unity, and power, to associated Christians. God set my mind and pen in motion. In 2002, I published *Martial Arts: The Christian Way*. Shortly thereafter, I started an online network with directories linking to every Christian martial arts homepage, program, school, and association that I knew about, and launched a major Christian martial arts program at my church. A non-profit association called Karate for Christ International was a big help to me in this process.

In 2003, membership in Karate for Christ International soared and a number of martial arts youth ministries popped up around the United States. I started receiving phone calls and email messages from pastors asking me about ways they could combine various forms of martial arts with Christian ministry and outreach. Since no other program that I knew of operated in the same way, and most interjected Christian teachings sporadically, I knew I was facing a real challenge. I began to pray about it, hoping for a simpler way than people having to form their own styles and systems, which can be very time-consuming. I believed that God had a way to use any martial arts style and system to raise Christians up in a like manner. Faithfully, God gave me such a vision.

God showed me His image of a Christian martial artist. I saw the great warriors of the Old Testament, the Disciples of the New Testament, all the major teachings of Christian life and service. I saw God's image of a Christian soldier, equipped with His glory and power to flee from temptation and fight against the devil and his legions of demons. I saw Christ as the Master of an army of Christian Black Belts preparing bodies, minds, and souls for everlasting Christian life and service. I saw the unchurched, young and mature Christians, and even Christian leaders growing through martial arts training. I saw a great ministry that God was birthing.

Then, it struck me. In society, black belts have a reputation of being strong, fearless, balanced, self-controlled, disciplined, and honorable, of high ethical and moral character. They are also considered leaders worthy of respect. This is what drives most martial artists to reach black-belt level and go beyond; it isn't so much the physical expertise as it is the respect and recognition they receive. In a similar manner, God wanted to establish the Christian black belt to be a trained warrior, worthy of respect, and physically, mentally, and spiritually equipped in the Christian faith.

I believe that God wants Christian men and women to rise up in strength and embrace His Way as traditional martial artists have embraced the ways of their masters. The Father desires His children to follow the one and only true Master, Jesus Christ, and strive to be more like Him because of the respect and honor that His name brings. God has already birthed a unique worldwide Christian martial arts ministry; now, He wants to build and refine it for purposes that we cannot even fathom. In His Way, the Christian Way, there is one path and the greatest warrior that ever lived walked that path.

In The Christian Way, the major teachings of Christian life and service are Salvation, loving God with body, mind, and soul, loving our neighbors as ourselves, the Fruit of the Spirit, the Full Armor of God, the Great Commission and bringing it all together in life and service. As Christian martial artists, the Bible is our training manual; its words and principles are integrated into our beings daily; our Master is the Lord Jesus Christ; and our goal is righteousness. In The Christian Way, it doesn't matter where we are in our walk or when we begin martial arts training. We can be very mature in our faith or brand new believers. As Christians, we are always learning and growing in the Lord.

The Bible is the Living Word of God, and He never stops revealing truth through it. "All Scripture is God-breathed and is useful for teaching, rebuking, correcting and training in righteousness" (2 Tim. 3:16). You can learn something from a Bible teaching when you're 18 years old and you can learn something altogether new from the same teaching when you're 60. A great example of this is Bugs Bunny cartoons. We loved them as kids, and we love them as adults; we catch different jokes and see new things in the same cartoon we may have watched ten times throughout life. Our brains can only understand what God prepares them to learn.

Chapter 4

ABOUT MARTIAL ARTS STYLES

There are different ways
God works in our lives,
but it is the same God who
does the work through all of us.

~ 1 Corinthians 12:6, NLT

There are so many martial arts styles; it would be impossible to cover all of them in this chapter, or even in a book! Thus, only some of the most popular styles are described here. They all involve distinct physical training, and they are all valuable in different ways and worth the time and energy to learn (if you so desire). Moreover, all of these styles can be tied to the Christian Way. The diverse techniques and movements are simply different physical expressions of the same path or way in Christ Jesus. Remember, the Christian Way is not physical techniques; it's spiritual growth.

Although some martial artists stick to one or two styles, others learn many. Different styles tend to complement each other and sharpen a student's overall skills. A martial artist who knows karate, judo, jujitsu, hapkido, and taekwondo is well equipped in the sport's arena and on the street. You have a broader perspective on effectiveness of different techniques in an array of styles. Although distinctions between them are few, different styles are valuable and distinguishable in distinct ways.

Styles tend to focus primarily on either sport or self-defense, but not both. Some of the most popular martial sports are judo and taekwondo. The martial artists from these styles usually spend a great deal of their energy preparing for competition. Although you learn self-defense, your techniques are not as street-practical as those of martial artists in styles that, for the most part, focus on defending themselves. On the other hand, styles that focus on self-defense are street-practical but not always sport-like. In these styles, you may miss the benefits that come from individual and team competition.

Styles also tend to be primarily "hard" or "soft." Hard styles focus on speed and power. The aim of these styles is typically to oppose an opponent's oncoming force. Soft styles, on the other hand, focus on skill and technique. The aim of these styles is not to oppose, but rather to redirect an opponent's oncoming force. Most styles are not totally hard or soft; they are a mixture of both in which one is usually dominant. A balance of hard and soft techniques improves a martial artist's form, speed, power, and overall preparedness in self-defense.

In terms of structure, it's important to remember that martial arts come from cultures that value honor and respect. This is a good thing because it teaches us how to be honorable and respectful of ourselves, others, and most importantly to God. Coming to class with a clean and pressed uniform, never putting our belts on the floor, bowing to other students and instructors during instruction, and addressing your fellow classmates as Mr. and Ms. are the ways you honor your life and the lives of those around you. It's also the way you honor God, with an appreciative and thankful heart.

Although historically it has not been the case, today martial arts styles have a colorful array of belt ranks. These belts typically range from light to dark as you progress through the arts. A black belt signifies your readiness to begin serious training. Black belt is the end of what is basic and the beginning of what is advanced. This is why the numeric system associated with the colored belt rankings decrease from white belt to black belt and increase after that (8th degree white; 7th degree yellow; 6th degree orange...1st degree black; 2nd degree black; 3rd degree black, etc.).

Rank plays an important role in the classroom. Students line up according to their belt ranks, treat higher-ranking students and instructors with respect, and acquire teaching privileges as they progress. Belt rank is a symbol of physical, mental, and spiritual development in the martial arts and the Christian faith. It's an outward expression of your personal growth as Christian soldiers in the martial arts. It means that you have progressed in some combination of physical, mental, and spiritual knowledge and have certain skills that you can pass on to others in the classroom and in life.

Rank does not indicate that you are any more developed than any other person; it's a sign of personal growth. Bodies, minds, and souls are all different and unique, according to God's design. Physically, not everyone's up-block will look the same and not everyone will have a fantastic sidekick, but everyone will earn rank for a belt if they know and do what is required. Mentally, not everyone will think alike or interpret the Bible in the same way, but if they do what is required, and challenge themselves to grow, they will earn rank. Spiritually, lower ranking students may be much more developed than higher-ranking students; those who challenge themselves to grow acquire rank. God never stops revealing, amen!

As you may have guessed, in the Christian Way, it doesn't matter where you are in terms of your faith or martial arts skills; you enter training as a white belt. You might ask, "I've been a pastor for several years, so does that mean I have to follow the spiritual curriculum?" Yes, even the most spiritually fit people continue to work out their salvation (Phil. 2:12) and therefore can learn and grow spiritually at each belt rank.

In a like manner, you might ask, "I have a brown belt already in this style, so don't I enter as a brown belt?" No, in the Christian Way, the physical techniques you learn can always be improved and your objective is to simultaneously challenge your body, mind, and soul on a personal level. It doesn't matter if you have been in ministry for 50 plus years, or have 100 black belt degrees; you are still like newborn babies to God, your Father. He wants you to grow up.

Martial arts classes typically begin with a formal bow, a Bible study/devotion, and a short prayer led by the head instructor. Sometimes classes set aside time for meditation with quiet focus on Jesus Christ. Shortly thereafter, the instructor leads students in a warm-up and stretch-out session to prepare the body for training.

After the body is warm and loose, students learn and practice a variety of martial arts techniques. You may learn blocks, punches, strikes, kicks, falls, rolls, breaks, street defense, grappling, kata, or kumite. After learning new techniques, you practice them daily, on your own, to remember and make the coordination a natural response. At the end of practice, you and the other students pray, bow out, and applaud.

Aikido

Aikido means "way of harmony" in Japanese. It's used to disable an attacker without exerting much force. The aikidoka (aikido practitioner) usually does not initiate an attack; instead, he/she waits for an attack and then responds in harmony. In other words, if an attacker throws a punch, the aikidoka steps back from the punch, grabs the attacker's arm, and pulls the person forward, using the attacker's own force against him. As a result, the attacker loses his balance and the aikidoka is able to take control of the situation.

Aikidokas study several different kinds of techniques. First, they learn how to fall correctly to avoid injury, as aikido is an art that requires a great deal of tumbling and rolling. Then they proceed to basic immobilizations such as wrist twists, wrist turns, and elbow locks. Aikidokas are able to take control of attackers by twisting and turning the opponents' wrists and pressuring the elbow joints beyond ordinary range of motion. The principle strategy is to move out of the line of attack, throw an attacker off balance by way of harmonic force, and apply some sort of immobilization. Movements are circular and flow smoothly throughout practice, much like a poetic dance.

Aikidokas wear hakamas (large pant-like skirts) and use staffs, wooden swords, and rubber knives to illustrate movements and teach defense against attacks. Precise timing and deftly applied force are necessary to perform such complex techniques. On a national level, Aikido is considered a soft martial style with a focus on self-defense rather than on sport.

Capoeira

Capoeira is a unique martial art that does not fit into any of the historical categories found in this book. Although its roots trace back to African dance, it was actually developed in Brazil by slaves attempting to protect themselves from the cruelty of their masters. Interestingly enough, the slave runners never knew about capoeira because the slaves tricked them into thinking their martial practice was just dance.

The capoeira practitioner learns many techniques that involve amazing acrobatics such as cartwheels, flips, and handstands, as well as more outright self-defense techniques like escapes, head butts, kicks, and sweeps. These techniques are practiced in the roda de capoeira, a game in which the capoeiristas (capoeira practitioners) form a circle and send two players to the middle. These two players then engage in a dance-like fight, each aiming to take over the space and the other player by way of mobility and precision as opposed to force.

In the early 1970s, capoeira became an official Brazilian sport. More than a sport, however, it represents a plethora of culture and history in Brazil. In addition to being a martial art, a sport, and a dance, capoeira is a free form of play. It's also an excellent exercise in terms of developing strength, flexibility, and endurance. Students are encouraged to work within their own range of abilities and there is less emphasis placed on rank than in other forms of martial arts. Capoeira is also considered a soft style.

Hapkido

Hapkido means the "way of harmony" in Korean. A Hapkido practitioner usually does not initiate an attack; instead, he/she waits for an attack and then responds in harmony. By putting pressure on certain skeletal joints and points, the Hapkido practitioner gains control over an attacker by using limited force and by using the attacker's own power against himself. This art is a combination of many martial arts styles, including aikido, kung fu, judo, and taekwondo.

The hapkido student learns how to defend against grabs, punches, kicks, and weapons. Similar to aikido, techniques usually take the path of least resistance, and incorporate joint locks and body throws to control an attacker. They may also include strikes, punches, and dynamic kicking techniques similar to taekwondo. Hapkido practitioners redirect attacks and follow through with offensive techniques to keep attackers from striking repeatedly.

Practitioners wear loose white suits, similar to those used in karate, and practice barefoot on hardwood floors. Because hapkido is Korean, it's often taught in conjunction with taekwondo and is very popular around the world. It's unique because it requires limited strength to execute techniques and control an attacker. Hapkido can be incorporated with any other style to enhance one's level of skills and training. Hapkido is a soft and hard martial art and is typically more focused on self-defense than on sport.

Jiujitsu

Jiujitsu means "gentle art" in Japanese and is considered to be the grandfather of aikido and judo. It uses both armed and unarmed techniques of the samurai. It's one of the most popular and practical martial arts today. Jiujitsu is different from karate and taekwondo in that it uses wrestling-like holds (grappling) to control an attacker, rather than using punches and kicks to incapacitate.

Jiujitsu practitioners learn how to perform striking, kicking, grappling, joint locking, and dislocation techniques. They also learn how to throw and break limbs much like ancient samurai. For about a century, jiujitsu has been used to train military and police officials. It's full of basic defense principles and is a good form of supplemental training to any martial arts style. It also trains in defense against weapons such as knives and guns. Brazilian jiujitsu is known to be especially effective in street self-defense. The secret, as they say, is to fight on the ground.

Typically, jiujitsu practitioners wear white suits similar to those worn in karate. Although it has traditionally focused on self-defense, it's evolving into a competitive sport and is popular in Hollywood films and on television. Because it was historically known as a killing art used in war, it's considered both hard and soft in nature. It's soft because it emphasizes grappling, throwing, and rolling much more than outright striking.

Judo

Judo means "gentle way" in Japanese and comes from the ancient martial art of jiujitsu. It's used to skillfully turn an attacker's own strength against him by developing skill, technique, and timing as opposed to strength. A judoka (judo practitioner) becomes proficient in throwing and wrestling-like techniques to defend against an attacker.

The first thing a judoka learns is how to fall correctly to avoid injury. Judokas are known for their ability to fall from great heights with minimal bodily damage. In addition to falling, the judoka learns the more popular techniques of the sport such as throwing, grappling, and choking, as well as joint locks. Judo is a refinement of jiujitsu, but is oriented more towards competition than self-defense. Skill and timing is emphasized over brute strength and are essential to the makeup of Judo. Students learn how to give way, rather than execute force, to overcome an attacker. Flexibility and balance are important to the techniques.

Typically, judokas wear gis (loose-fitting cotton suits) and practice barefoot on special mats. Judo is the oldest martial sport in history and the first Eastern martial art to be accepted into the Olympic Games (1964). Consequently, it has rules like any competitive sport. It's considered a soft style of the martial arts and is regarded as being safe, as well as a great deal of fun. People from all different age groups, with all different abilities, train in judo (including people who are physically challenged). In fact, judo is said to have many benefits for the visually impaired.

Karate

Karate means "empty hand" in Japanese and is primarily used to combat an attacker in self-defense. Its linear offensive techniques are considered hard in nature and its circular defensive techniques are considered soft. Thus, it offers a nice blend of the different principles that make up martial arts. Karatekas (karate practitioners) are usually fit; a good workout is usually indicated by a wet uniform and belt after class.

Karatekas study several different kinds of techniques including escapes, blocks, punches, kicks, and combinations. They practice what they learn through kata (a memorized sequence of techniques), kumite (sparring with a partner), combinations, and simulated street attacks. The karateka is required to display respect in relationships and control in the classroom by demonstrating skill, speed, and power without making physical contact with the opponent. It's truly amazing to execute a kick at 70mph and stop it within a half-inch to a quarter-inch of an opponent's nose!

Karatekas wear gis (loose fitting suits) and practice barefoot in dojos (traditional training halls) with mirrors and hard floors. They work their arms as much as their legs and develop a balanced, muscular physique. Weapons are typically used only to illustrate defensive techniques against attacks. Overall, karate is considered a competitive and safe sport, as well as a complete system of self-defense.

Kung Fu

Kung fu means "an acquired skill" in Cantonese and it describes literally hundreds of Chinese martial forms and styles. A modern-day term that better describes the nature of kung fu is wu shu, which means "martial art" in Chinese. Kung fu is the oldest of all martial forms and is made up of both hard and soft styles. Two of the most famous hard styles are shaolin and wing chun (the first martial art learned by Bruce Lee), and two of the most famous soft styles are t'ai chi and pa kua.

Hard styles of kung fu employ strength and power through karate-like techniques and more. These techniques include punches, kicks, and throws, as well as acrobatics like flips, handsprings, cartwheels, and somersaults. Many of the fighting systems and techniques come from the defensive and offensive moves of animals, including snakes, leopards, tigers, cranes, and dragons (the ancient name for dinosaurs).

Soft styles of kung fu employ slow flowing movements that develop force as opposed to strength. The practitioner focuses on relaxing the mind and body and then moving in harmony with respiration. Movements are practiced through memorized sequences known as "forms" and utilize nearly every part of the body from the bottom of the foot to the top of the head. Posture and breathing are extremely important.

Practitioners wear sams (loose tunic tops) with loose pants and soft shoes. The hard styles tend to be competitive, as they are more geared towards self-defense. The soft styles are performed mainly for the sake of health and wellness.

Taekwondo

Taekwondo means "the way of the foot and fist" in Korean, and is famous for its high, fast, and spinning kicks. Literally, tae means "to kick", kwon means "to punch", and do means "way". It's the most popular martial art in the world with some 40 million practitioners in 142 countries. Taekwondo is an artistic discipline that is pleasing to the eye; practitioners show a great deal of grace and attention to detail.

Practitioners learn how to punch, block, and kick, but they use their legs far more than any other part of the body. They practice what they learn through martial forms (memorized sequences of techniques) and free sparring. They also learn basic escapes and defense against weapons. Much emphasis is placed on breaking boards and bricks, among other things, and sparring. Breaking is a demonstration of focus, speed, and power, and sparring is technique in motion. Practitioners are encouraged to live by tenets such as courtesy, integrity, perseverance, and self-control in the classroom and in their lives.

Practitioners wear a loose white suit, known as a dobok, and practice barefoot on hardwood floors. Ranks are divided into ten *kup* (pupil) levels and nine *dan* (expert) levels. During sparring matches, they wear a lot of protective gear, as they make hard physical contact in competition. Taekwondo is a hard style and a competitive sport, and great emphasis is placed on tournament breaking and sparring. In 1980, it officially became an Olympic sport.

Tang Soo Do

Tang soo do means "way of the China hand" in Korean, and comes from the ancient art of Soo Bahk Do, as well as Northern and Southern China kung fu. In essence, tang so do is a classical Korean martial art that was influenced by the T'ang Dynasty of China. It's an artistic discipline that is pleasing to the eye; practitioners show a great deal of grace and attention to detail.

Practitioners learn empty hand and foot fighting, self-defense, and weapons, as well as high, jumping, and spinning kicks. Tang soo do is an art, not a competitive sport, and is based on classical form. Its purpose is to develop the mind, body, and soul to create a mature and balanced person. Much emphasis is placed on perfecting techniques through the art of breaking and sparring. The art of breaking demonstrates form, focus, speed, and power, and the art of sparring allows for practice of techniques.

Practitioners wear a loose white suit, known as a dobok, and practice barefoot on hardwood floors. Ranks are divided into *gup* (pupil) levels and *dan* (black belt) levels. Because sparring doesn't produce much contact, practitioners don't usually wear much protective gear. Tang Soo Do is hard and soft; the hard external influence comes from soo bahk do and the soft internal from the systems of Northern China. Both of these systems are noticeable in the forms of the art.

Chapter 5

Salvation and Eternal Life

May you always be filled with

the fruit of your salvation—

those good things that are

produced in your life by Jesus

Christ—for this will bring much

glory and praise to God.

~ Philippians 1:11, NLT

1. To Bow or Not to Bow

In martial arts class, we bow to our school, our instructors, and our fellow classmates, as a form of greeting and as a sign of respect. Just as men and women shake hands in the United States or exchange a kiss on the cheek in some Latin and European countries, people in various parts of East Asia bow when they encounter each other. Since martial arts came from East Asia, the cultural tradition of bowing came with it, and many Western martial artists observe the practice today.

Bowing has a larger, religious implication for Christian martial artists. It's a spiritual act and a symbolic expression of worship and honor for the Lord Jesus Christ. Various men and women are recorded in the Bible to have kneeled and bowed to God in worship, honor, and praise. In fact, the Word tells us that everyone shall one day bow down to Christ. While it's clear that we are not to worship idols (Lev. 26:1), it's God's will that Christians bow in their worship to the Master Jesus Christ and God (Phil. 2:10; Ps. 95:6; 2 Chr. 6:13, 14).

PRINCIPLE	Bow to each other in greeting and respect, but bow in worship only to the Master, Christ.
CODES	Romans 14:11
	Philippians 2:10
	James 4:10

2. Fear has a Purpose

Fear is a natural part of our human design that drives us to God. Not everyone believes this of course. Some believe we should not fear because the Bible says, "God is love" (1 John 4:8 NIV) and "There is no fear in love. But perfect love drives out fear" (1 John 4:18 NIV). These same people like to quote 2 Timothy 1:7, which tells us that God didn't give us a spirit of fear.

I know a black belt with panic disorder, who praises God and calls his disorder a gift. He's the founder of a major karate system and ranks as a highly esteemed and respected Christian martial artist. Had he not been fearful, he would never have come to the Lord. Just think about it, what might happen to little children if they weren't fearful of their parents? They most likely wouldn't grow up to become adults.

Sometimes I take my baby boy into the pool with me to relax. If I put him in a raft by himself to float, he gets frightened and starts crying and screaming for me to pick him up. When I take him into my arms, all his fear dissolves, even though we're both still in the water. He feels completely protected in my arms, and rightfully so, because I'm his mom, and if I weren't there to protect him, he could drown.

In the same way that my baby boy is afraid to be alone on a raft in a pool, we're afraid to be alone in various life circumstances. All we have to do when we're afraid is call out to our Father and He will pick us up and hold us close. Since we're completely protected in our Father's arms, we can handle even the most unbearable circumstances, and physical death can't separate us from Him. If we didn't have fear, we wouldn't thirst for God's protection and love, and would never know Him or eternal life.

God wants us to thirst long for Him, so that He can protect us and give us everything His heart desires. "For God so loved the world, that he gave his only begotten Son, that whosoever believeth in him should not perish, but have everlasting life" (John 3:16, KJV). As 1 John 4:18 tells us, there's no fear in God because fear drives us to Him, and He casts it out. In His arms, there's no reason to fear.

PRINCIPLE   Fear drives us to God.

CODES   Matthew 10:28
             Psalms 23:4
             Isaiah 66:13

3. True Freedom

As martial artists, we also train to escape captivity, and rescue others from it. Whether it's an assault, a robbery, a fight, a battle, abduction, or a war, our goal is freedom. For the Christian martial artist, freedom goes beyond the physical to the mental and the spiritual. It releases strongholds of every kind and breaks through the chains and shackles around the heart, mind, and soul. When true freedom comes, nothing can keep us from it or take it away.

Like the chains and shackles that bind man in prison and keep him from seeing the light of day, sin binds a man's heart, mind, and soul and keeps him from the only thing worth living for...a loving relationship with his Heavenly Father.

Jesus Christ came to set the captives free by removing sin from the lives of men and taking it upon Himself at the cross. Jesus already removed the chains and shackles on our lives; all we have to do is believe it, accept it, and receive it by giving our lives to Him, and letting Him work through us to do the will of the Father on earth.

Truly, Jesus Christ was the best martial artist ever to walk the planet and this is why we call Him Master. His most powerful weapon is truth. By believing, teaching, and living the truth, He set us all free from captivity. Truth brings freedom; lies bring bondage and captivity; it's as simple as that. Satan is the author and creator of lies, and by getting us to believe and accept his lies; we do certain things called sin, which robs, kills, and destroys. God is the author and creator of truth, and by getting us to believe and accept His truth, we do certain things that are righteous which give, save, build up, and bring eternal life.

We were made to live in freedom with our Author, Creator, and Heavenly Father; however, when Adam and Eve ate of the tree of the knowledge of good and evil, sin entered the world and man has been living in captivity ever since. Breaking free from sin and captivity requires that you invite the best martial artist that ever lived into your life to fight for and rescue your soul. God does not and cannot live in lies and sin. Have you ever tried to make a fish live outside of water? If so, you probably know what happens... it dies. Well, if God tried to live in lies and sin, He would die and so would we, since He is our Author and Creator. For this reason, God has to draw us out of sin to Him. He did all that He could do by sending his son to earth to experience the temptations of man die as the ultimate sacrifice and atonement for sin.

PRINCIPLE   Truth + Christ = Freedom

CODES   John 8:32
             Romans 6:22
             John 8:36

4. Good Fear and Bad Fear

As you may have gathered from the previous lessons, there are three different kinds of fears. There is (1) fear of God and what He'll do if we don't obey Him, (2) fear for our lives with respect to the things that can harm us on earth, and (3) fear in the face of God's purpose and plans. The first two fears are healthy gifts from God, but the third is not from God, it's actually sin.

The best way to illustrate these fears is to look at children and their parents. A young child, who doesn't use his karate on others because he is afraid of being spanked for breaking a rule, is wise and fearful "of" his parents. This type of fear protects him and others from getting hurt by things that he doesn't understand. Notice, he is not afraid of his parents as people (because he knows they love him), he is fearful of what they'll do if he disobeys or doesn't do as he is told.

A child who starts screaming when a strange dog approaches and licks her is fearful for her life and wants mom or dad to immediately pick her up and protect her. A child who falls off her bike and comes home crying with a scraped-up knee is fearful for her well-being and wants mom or dad to treat her knee and assure her it will be okay. This type of fear is a protective mechanism that God puts into our minds, so that we will seek safety and protection when threatened. It's God's way of keeping us alive and close to Him in chaos. It's also God's way of protecting our bodies, which are his temples.

Lastly, if a child refuses to obey his mom and dad because he is fearful of something they've asked him to do (like hug his Grandma Suzie, take a bath, or clean his closet), then he is disobeying his parents and committing a sin. Even though mom and dad told him it was okay and he would be protected, he refused to do their will because he didn't trust them, and instead, trusted his own feelings of fear. This type of fear keeps us from being the people that God created us to be and from doing the things that God asks us to do. It's the cause of disobedience to God. When we are fearful without reason, we don't trust God for our safety, and we are living in ourselves, instead of in Him.

PRINCIPLE	Some fear is God-given and some fear is sin. Regardless, we should obey God.
CODES	Ecclesiastes 12:13 John 14:15 Psalm 18:2

5. Salvation and Accountability

When I first became a Christian, I was told that Jesus Christ died for me, that salvation was free and could not be earned, and that all I had to do was ask Jesus to come into my heart and I'd be saved. However, my understanding of what I was told was not correct. First, I understood the word "free" to mean something that you get for nothing. Second, I had no concept of what it meant to ask Jesus into my heart. Third, I thought I didn't have to do anything but read my Bible and pray.

It didn't occur to me what the word "free" really meant until someone gave me a puppy of my very own. While the puppy didn't cost me any money, I wasn't getting something for nothing. I had to make it a bed, feed it, clean up its poop, take it for shots, walk it, groom it, and train it. It took a lot of time and energy, but I can honestly say it was well worth it all. Salvation is a similar, but comes with more responsibility. When we are saved, we are vowing to die to ourselves so that Christ can live through us. Baptism is a symbol of our salvation; we are buried with Christ into death so that we can rise with Him into eternal life (Rom 6). It's a huge, gigantic commitment.

When the Bible refers to the free gift of salvation, it means that God gives us the seeds, the water, the ground, and the sun to bear fruit. We have to plant the seeds, make sure they get enough water, allow time for them to grow into trees, reap the fruit that they produce, prepare the fruit, and then eat it. As you can see, it does NOT mean we get something for nothing. Much like Salvation, we believe that fruit will satisfy our hunger and so we do something to get it into our mouths and bellies on a daily basis. No matter how hard we believe that the fruit will satisfy our hunger, we would starve to death if we didn't do something to get it into our systems.

While some may say that all you have to do is believe in order to be saved, believing and doing go hand-in-hand (1 John 3:6-9). Believing that Jesus is the answer and asking Him into your heart nonchalantly is not enough; you must do everything you can, on a daily basis, to die to yourself and allow Christ to be resurrected and raised in you. Only God gives us new life and a new relationship with Him, but He has given us the responsibility of doing our part to make that new relationship grow. This means going to church, surrounding yourself with Christians, reading the Word, praying, and doing what God tells you to do. As Christians, our minds and bodies should be like free flowing streams for Christ to pour through, but they often get clogged and polluted with the junk that this world dumps in them. Everyday, we have to clean our steams, strain them, and remove the junk so that God can flow through us and use us as a vessel.

Like the most joyous things of life, Salvation takes responsibility. In martial arts training, we exercise hard and train to protect; we make sacrifices in time and energy, but it's worth every minute and ounce of sweat. Training, like Salvation, gives us strength, confidence, and endurance and helps us to enjoy our lives more fully. The big difference is that we can live our lives on earth and eternally without any martial arts training, but we can't really live without God. "It is written, That man shall not live by bread alone, but by every word of God" (Luke 4:4, KJV).

If you are not saved and you think you are fine, I challenge you to think again. Jesus is the only truth, way, and life (John 14:6). If you are saved, I challenge you to look at what your Salvation means to you and how much you've done in it. Believing and doing go hand-in-hand. Read James 2:14-26.

| PRINCIPLE | Salvation takes responsibility and is demonstrated by beliefs and deeds. |
| CODES | James 2:26 |

1 John 3:18
Matthew 7:21-27

6. Standing Firm

As a martial artist, you learn and practice stances for several reasons. A good solid stance (1) keeps you from being thrown off balance or knocked down; (2) helps you move and execute your techniques faster and stronger; (3) protects your legs from being sprained or broken; and (4) lowers your center of gravity so that you can take control of your opponents with more ease, without getting hurt. As a Christian, you apply these same principles to your faith. God tells us to stand firm and keep a strong grip on the teachings of the Bible (2 Thess. 2:15). Just as good stances form the foundation by which you execute all your martial arts techniques, standing firm is the foundation of your Christian faith. With a good, strong stance, you can use the Full Armor of God and protect yourself against the schemes of the devil (Eph. 6:11).

In Ephesians 6:13-14, Paul tells us to stand, to stand our ground, and to stand firm (NIV), before he goes into an explanation of the Armor of God. So, as you learn and practice your stances in martial arts, be patient and don't slack in your training. When you do your front stance, your front knee should be bent and your back leg locked. Sure, it hurts, but you must train your muscles to hold the stance. "No discipline is enjoyable while it is happening—it is painful! But afterward there will be a quiet harvest of right living for those who are trained in this way. So, take a new grip with your tired hands and stand firm on your shaky legs. Mark out a straight path for your feet. Then those who follow you, though they are weak and lame, will not stumble and fall but will become strong" (Heb. 12:11-13 NLT).

PRINCIPLE	Standing firm is your foundation, in martial arts and in God.
CODES	2 Corinthians 1:21
	2 Chronicles 20:20
	Proverbs 12:7
	Ephesians 6:11

7. Working out your Salvation

Submitting to Christ is the first step in the training of a Christian martial artist. No matter when you are saved, what church you go to, or where you are in your faith, this chapter will help you in the working out of your salvation with fear and trembling (Phil. 2:12 NIV). The Bible tells us to "Serve the Lord with fear and rejoice with trembling" (Ps. 2:11 NIV). It also says "The fear of the Lord is the beginning of wisdom" (Prov. 9:10 NIV) and "The fear of the Lord is a fountain of life, turning a man from the snares of death" (Prov. 14:27 NIV).

My son fears his father and me. While he comes to us to seek protection, he fears how we might react if he doesn't do what he is told to do, or if he does something that he knows he isn't supposed to do. He doesn't understand how our rules can exist for his protection; he only knows who he has to stand accountable to if he breaks them and gets caught, or if he breaks them and gets hurt and then has to come to his father or me to make the "ouchy" hurt go away. We always receive him with love but we still have to punish him when he does something wrong, so that he'll learn not to do it again.

In the same way that my son fears his father and me, we should fear God, our Father. If my son didn't fear his father and me, then he'd do whatever he pleased without caring about the consequences, whether it meant being caught or getting hurt. This could prove very destructive; he could drink poison or run in front of a car. When he gets older, and starts his martial arts training, he could be puffed up with pride, break the law, hurt someone, or ruin his life through some other means. The fear of God protects and saves our lives (Prov. 14:27). If we know what is best, we fear Him and His rules even if we don't understand.

PRINCIPLE   Fear of God protects our Salvation.

CODES   Proverbs 1:7
             Proverbs 16:6
             Proverbs 19:23
             Proverbs 22:4

8. Your Uniform

You are here today because you are God's son or daughter; you desire to train your body and mind in His righteousness. Nevertheless, have you ever thought about why you wear a white uniform? Uniforms come in all different colors, from yellow to blue to red, but you wear white. Do you know why you wear white? As a follower of the Master Jesus Christ, you wear white on the outside of your body to represent the white on the inside that has washed you clean.

Unlike many other martial artists, you are a Christian martial artist. You are a member of God's family, but also a soldier in His army, and you fight for righteousness. You are God's vessel and temple and He uses you and your body to accomplish His good things on earth (1 Cor. 6:19). When Jesus was close to the Father and the Kingdom of God, He was clothed in white. The Bible is full of scriptures that tell us that the color white is the Lord's; He uses it to represent that which is His.

While often called white, yellow, red, or black, skin is none of these colors. White people range from peachy to tan and black people range from tan to dark brown, so do not think because you are called "white" in modern-day society that you are any holier than your black brother or sister. You are not. The scriptures in the Bible have nothing to do with the color of your skin, but with the clothing that you wear in God's army and kingdom and what that clothing represents. White clothing represents the righteousness of God, given freely to us through Jesus Christ. We have never seen any white with our human eyes as white as the righteousness of the Lord.

PRINCIPLE	The color white represents God's righteousness.
CODES	Mark 9:1-3
	Revelation 3:5
	Revelation 7:14

Chapter 6

Physical–Mental–Spiritual Relationship

*The most important
commandment is this:
'Hear, O Israel! The Lord our God
is the one and only Lord.
And you must love
the Lord your God
with all your heart,
all your soul,
all your mind,
and all your strength.'*

~ Mark 12: 29-30, NLT

9. Physical-Mental-Spiritual Love

"And thou shalt love the Lord thy God with all thy heart, and with all thy soul, and with all thy mind, and with all thy strength: this is the first commandment" (Mark 12:30, KJV). Any way you look at this scripture, it tells us to love God with our whole beings: mentally, physically, and spiritually. How do we show God that we love Him? We obey His Word (John 14:15). The Bible tells us exactly what to do with our mental, physical, and spiritual selves.

We are to honor God with our bodies and treat them as God's temples (1 Cor. 3:16; 6:19-20). This concept is easy enough to figure out by looking at how people treat religious temples on earth (the church building for example). People generally keep their church building clean and use it to bring them and others closer to God. People worship, honor, and glorify God in the church building. In the same way, we should keep our bodies clean (inside and out) and use them to get closer to God. Our bodies are the vehicles by which we worship, honor, and glorify God. Ultimately, it's not the church's building that God is concerned with; it's our bodies through which we serve Him.

Just as we love God physically, we are to love Him mentally. We are to use our minds according to God's purpose and think upon certain things (Phil. 4:8-9). It means discipleship; it means disciplining our thought processes. The Bible tells us to get rid of our old thoughts and attitudes and renew our minds in Christ. (Eph. 4:22-23). "If your sinful nature controls your mind, there is death. But if the Holy Spirit controls your mind, there is life and peace" (Rom 8:6, NLT). There are many forces fighting for control of your mind (Rom 7:23-

24), but your attitude should always be the same as that of Jesus (Phil. 2:5).

Spiritually, we love God by producing the Fruit of the Spirit in our lives (Gal. 5:22-23). The Bible tells us that a good tree produces good fruit (Matt. 7:8). It also tells us that we can identify people by the kind of fruit that they produce (Matt. 7:20). Consequently, the Fruit of the Spirit is more than a byproduct of the Christian way; it's a secret code used to identify Christians. Jesus tells us how to keep this code: "Remain in me, and I will remain in you. No branch can bear fruit by itself; it must remain in the vine" (John 15:4, NIV). Read John 15:1-17 for an excellent description of how Fruit is produced in our lives.

PRINCIPLE   We love God with our entire beings by
             keeping his commands.
CODES   1 Thessalonians 4:4
             Philippians 2:2
             1 Corinthians 6:17

10. The Body-Mind-Soul Connection to God

As human beings, we separate the body, mind, and soul into different boxes. Categorizing things is just our way of making sense of the world. We think of nutrition as being good for the body, academics as being good for the mind, and Christian fellowship as being good for the soul. In reality, the body, mind, and soul are interconnected; what is good for one is good for all, and what is bad for one is bad for all. Stress comes into our lives through the mind, but it has serious consequences on the body and soul. Alcohol comes through the body, but it has strong effects on the mind and soul.

Just as we make sense of the world by categorizing, we also make sense of it through analogies. The following analogy explains the body-mind-soul connection to God.

- The vehicle is our body. It takes gas and oil to go, maintenance to keep going, will last a long time if we take care of it, sometimes needs replacement parts, and will eventually wear out and die. For as long as it lasts, it takes us wherever we want to go, so long as there is a road to get there.

- The driver is our mind. He determines what type of gas and oil to put into the vehicle, how it's cared for, where it will go, and what it will go through. If he takes good care of the vehicle, it will last him a long time; if not, then it will wear out quickly.

- The passenger is our soul. She is entirely dependent on the driver and the vehicle, how they work together and where they end up going. While the passenger can make suggestions, she is not in control and must submit to the driver and the vehicle.

- The road is our spirit. The Human Spirit consists of all kinds of roads that take us many different places but lead us nowhere. The Holy Spirit is one very narrow, but picturesque road that leads us to the Father. This road was built by Jesus Christ, and He died in the process. Those who take this road today must pay a toll in living sacrifice.

- The road map is the Word of God. It will direct us and tell us which roads to take on our journey through life.

As Christian martial artists, we need to be aware of the journey we take with our bodies, minds, and souls. Our minds should be driving us on the road of the Holy Spirit and our bodies should be transporting us there.

PRINCIPLE Align your body and mind to take your soul home to the Father.

CODES   Matthew 6:22
         Philippians 2:5

11. Striking a Balance

One of the first things that we learn in martial arts is balance. We have to be able to hold our leg in the air before we can begin to develop form, speed, and power in our kicks. If we don't have good balance, we fall and get hurt. Life is the same way; if we don't have good balance, we fall and injure ourselves. God created us in His image as mental, physical, spiritual, and social beings. He commanded us to love Him and our neighbors in a balanced way (Mark 12:30) and to do things in moderation (Eccl. 7:15-22). He did this for our own well-being and health.

There was time in my life when I spent more than 15 hours a day at the computer doing research and writing; I didn't eat well, I didn't get any exercise, and I spent very little time with my family and friends. My muscles grew weak, my abdomen started to cramp, and my back tightened up into all sorts of painful knots. I lost weight, my hair and nails grew brittle and my family and friends remarked about how pale and frail I looked. I was having problems at work and the stress level in my life was high, so I wasn't thinking properly.

I was always cranky, too. Never in my life had I been in such poor health.

I saw all sorts of specialists for my ailments and it wasn't until I went to a gastrointestinal specialist that I knew I had to change. When I was sitting in the office, I noticed all the elder people around me with problems. Some had Crone's Disease, some had ulcers and tumors, and some could hardly even walk. I picked up some literature and starting reading about what can happen when a person doesn't eat properly and get enough fiber and I cringed. I don't know what happened, but something changed me on the inside and God showed me that the cure was not doctors and drugs, in my case; it was a balanced and healthy lifestyle. I made myself a schedule to go jogging 3 days a week, took up martial arts again, started eating healthy, and set aside playtime with my family.

Today, I am healthy and strong and my outlook on life is a happy, positive one. I thank God every day for turning me around on the dangerous path I was walking. Imbalance in life is like poison acid that eats away slowly at the bones without your even knowing it. It's critical that we care for the precious bodies, minds, souls, and loved ones that God gives us in this life. If we don't we may lose them.

PRINCIPLE	Mental, physical, spiritual, and social balance reaps health.
CODES	Ecclesiastes 7:16-18
	Proverbs 30:8-9

12. About Physical Discomfort

In the modern-day western world, physical discomfort is generally intolerable (especially as we age). If an ache or pain comes along, we pop a pill; if our car breaks down, we stay home; if a nutritious food doesn't taste good, we don't eat it. Learning to cope with aches and pains, walking and/or bicycling as transportation, and eating bland foods that don't stimulate all of our taste buds is unheard of in society. Despite the fact that the longevity of our lives has increased, the quality of our lives has decreased. People are not stronger and more able than their ancestors were and they don't know how to live with discomfort.

When I lived in Africa, I was amazed by the physical stamina of the people. I'll never forget the one time I went to a Christian conference. I took a two-hour taxi ride, but many who couldn't afford a taxi. Instead of catching the conference another year when they had more money, they left a couple of days early to hike over and through the mountains, barefoot, with no food, no water, and no money. Yet, God provided for them every step of the way. Not only did they demonstrate great physical stamina, but also great faith. What amazed me the most about the African Christians was their ability to experience the joy and peace of the Lord in extreme discomfort.

Physical discomfort, in and of itself, is not a problem, but being unable to do what God calls us to do because of physical discomfort is a problem. The Lord calls us to defend the name of Jesus (Acts 4:1-14; Phil. 2:9-11) and to be an ambassador for Christ (2 Cor. 5:17-21). The Lord would like us to get beyond physical self to a spiritual plateau that is immoveable by Satan or man. Take Job for instance; Job suffered from a terrible sickness in his body, but he still stood high and mighty in the Lord. No matter what Satan did to Job, he couldn't move Job's love and faithfulness toward the Lord. Job rose above the physical life to a much closer walk with God.

Look at all the great men of the Bible and what they went through. As a young man, Jesus Himself suffered from physical discomfort to help Him submit His entire being to the Father and prepare for ministry. Following His baptism by John, He was led by the Spirit into the wilderness on foot and then stayed there alone for forty days and nights with no food (Matthew 4). He resisted the longing of the flesh to eat and He refused to give in to the various temptations of the devil. Then, He began His ministry and called the first disciples. At the end of His ministry, Jesus suffered extreme pain because of the cruelty of man, unto His death, but His heart was never on Himself. Instead, it was on the well-being of His persecutors, asking His father to forgive them (Luke 23:34).

Martial artists have a reputation of purposely building physical stamina. In some arts, people walk on broken glass, in others they toughen up their knuckles by hitting things repeatedly. As part of my black belt test, I had to run barefoot for two miles in the snow. Actually, I never had to do it (that's a secret so hush hush). My instructor told me that I had to do it if I wanted my black belt, and then when I started, he told me to turn around and go back. He just wanted to see if I was willing to do whatever it took to reach my goal. It reminds me of when God tested Abraham by asking him to kill his son, Isaac, just to see if Abraham would obey (Gen.

22). As Christian martial artists, our goal is not only rank, but more importantly, to fulfill God's purpose for our lives.

PRINCIPLE	Don't allow physical discomfort keep you from doing God's will.
CODES	1 Peter 2:20-21
	1 Peter 4:13

13. The Temple

According to martial arts tradition, the dojo, or dojang is a temple for training. It's treated with respect and honor and must be kept clean in order for instructors and students to work out in it. A church building is also a temple; it must be cleaned and maintained on a regular basis in order for a group of people to hold their services within.

As a Christian, your body is a temple (1 Cor. 6:19), a place where God lives, and dwells. Your role is to make sure that your temple is clean and pure, suitable for the Lord God. God cannot live in dirty, sinful filth. He can only live in clean temples that are washed by the blood of Jesus of all impurities; in Him, there is no sin (1 John 3:5).

Interesting enough, God doesn't live in church; He lives in the people who go to church. "The God who made the world and everything in it is the Lord of heaven and earth and does not live in temples built by hands" (Act 17:24, NIV). His people are His temples, not the buildings they construct, or the works they complete. In your body is where He dwells.

As Christian martial artists, we devote and dedicate our bodies to God's temples. We beat our bodies and make them a slave to Christ so that we won't be disqualified for God's presence (1 Cor. 9:27). After all, it's great pleasure and honor to host the Lord of All, King of Kings, in our bodies. He cannot and will not live and dwell in filth.

PRINCIPLE   Host God in your temple; it's a glorious honor.

CODES   Psalm 27:4
            1 Corinthians 3:16
            2 Corinthians 6:16

14. Building Endurance

It's a steamy hot day and sweat is pouring off your forehead. Your t-shirt is wet and your eyes sting from salty sweat beads dripping down your face. Your opponent is coming at you full force with lots of kicks and punches and you are trying hard just to block and stay on your feet. Your techniques are slow and your breath is heavy; you feel like giving up the match, but you don't. Instead, you hang in there and pray for victory, with a desire, a goal, and a dream to win! If you can just win the fight, you will be able to rest in the prize. The crowd will cheer and your friends and relatives will be proud because you came out as number one.

Endurance is the length of time that we are able to keep going under dire circumstances; it's what keeps us sparring in matches when we are tired and out of breath. Consequently, we try to build endurance with hard training. The more endurance we can build, the longer we will be able to fight in a match and the greater the probability that we will wear out our opponent and win. Endurance is critical in martial arts but is also the secret ingredient to success and purposeful living; the more we push ourselves to be and do as Christians living in the present, the more we will become in the future.

God wants us to build endurance in life in the same way that we build it in martial arts class. Life has a way of throwing things at us that are hard to deal with, but we must keep going. While sometimes we feel like giving up, God always provides a way for us to keep going. He doesn't want us to cash in the cow, He wants us to tough it out and endure no matter what the circumstances might be. He knows that if we forfeit the match in life, we will not win. He wants to cheer us all to victory and give us the prize. While a match in martial arts is between two or more people, the match of the Christian life is within you alone. Read the Book of Job for an extreme example of endurance.

PRINCIPLE   Endurance is the key to Christian victory.

CODES   Hebrews 12:1
               1 Corinthians 9:24-27

15. Exercising our Spirituality

Getting in shape physically helps us to get in shape spiritually. Paul wrote, "I beat my body and make it a slave so that after I have preached to others, I myself will not be disqualified for the prize" (1 Cor. 9:27, NIV). In other words, Paul trained his body to diligently live by and do the work of Jesus Christ. The Bible tells us that we should have the same attitude that Christ had about bodily suffering; "he who has suffered in his body is done with sin" (1 Pet 4:1, NIV). After all, if our bodies are not trained and are too tired to do all that God asks us to do, then how can we live in obedience?

In martial arts class, we do many difficult exercises and our bodies suffer. We stretch, we strengthen, we build endurance, and we execute techniques that take energy and sweat. We work hard, but the payoff is great. Healthy, strong, flexible bodies are the result of our training. When done within God's realm, physical hardship builds spiritual strength (Col. 1:10-12). It prepares us to do the will of God, whatever it may be. God told Noah to build an ark (Gen. 6-7), and He told Moses to deliver the Israelites (Ex. 3-4), neither of which were small tasks. Have you ever thought about how much wood Noah had to chop and how many nails he had to hammer to build an ark that was 450 feet long, 75 feet wide, and 45 feet high?

God asks us to do things that take enormous strength and stamina, so it's logical to assume that He wants us to train our bodies and discipline them to do His will. The Holy Bible tells us this fact. So, the next time your arms feel like jelly from doing pushups or your belt is wet from a hard work out, remember why you're doing it. For everything you do, you should do for the glory of God (1 Cor. 10:31). Rest assured that when you are in the condition that God wants you to be in, you'll be better equipped to fulfill the plan that He has for your life.

PRINCIPLE	Physical hardship builds spiritual strength through Christ.
CODES	Philippians 4:13
	Hebrews 12:1

16. Life is in the Blood

As a defender of life, have you ever wondered where life resides? Certainly, it resides in the body, but specifically, it resides in the blood (Lev. 17:11). The blood is not life, but the blood carries the life of every living creature. The brain tells the heart to pump blood through the entire body because the blood is what gives it life. Have you ever accidentally cut off the blood supply to your arm or leg? Did it feel all tingly and motionless inside? If so, it's because for a moment there was no life in that part of your body. Once you restored the blood to the lifeless part, the feeling came back and you could control and move it again. No scientist will ever be able to explain how the blood carries life, but it does.

The bones, the flesh, and the organs that make up the body have a very important purpose with respect to the life in the blood. Their job is to work together to transport the life in the blood for a specific amount of time on earth. In doing so, they temporarily collaborate with the earth's environment to provide an experience, or journey, for a greater purpose. Have you ever thought about just how much your life on earth is dependent on environmental conditions? Without the sun, the rain, and the soil, there would be no greenery, no oxygen, no food, and no drink. Without gravity, it would be impossible to build homes and make do to survive. Without at least some of the five senses, there would be no way to interpret or make sense of the world enough to live in it. It's not a coincidence that the body is designed this way.

So the blood carries life and the body is a temporary vessel by which life journeys the earth. God designed it this way for a purpose. Unfortunately, many people are caught up in the pursuit of life instead of the pursuit of purpose. The biggest businesses in the world claim to have the secrets of life. People spend lots of time and money on diets, exercises, medications, vitamins, herbs, creams, bracelets, surgery, and much more to preserve and prolong their lives on earth. They think living longer is the purpose of life and so try to draw out this misguided purpose through a seemingly endless search for the fountain of youth. Such people are lost sheep without a Shepherd. As Christians, we take care of our bodies not to preserve our youthfulness, but to fulfill a God-given purpose on earth. We understand that life can extend beyond our time on earth, too.

Being Christian martial artists, we stretch to help the blood move through the entire body and we build endurance to help the heart pump blood efficiently. We strengthen our muscles to withstand suffering and we eat right to help protect our blood from toxins that cause illness. Taking care of our body doesn't prolong the natural aging process, and it isn't a foolproof barrier for sickness and disease, it helps us to accomplish our purpose on earth. From a spiritual perspective, we know that without Christ, the life that flows through our blood and body is contaminated with sin and is headed for death. However, with Christ, the life that flows through our blood and body is purified and eternal. This is why in communion we drink the blood and eat the body of Christ (John 6:54); we openly accept Him as the Savior of our life.

PRINCIPLE   Your life is unseen and is in the blood. It temporarily travels through the body and its final destination is determined on the journey by a decision to either accept or deny Christ.

CODES	Leviticus 17:11
	Hebrews 9:22
	1 Peter 1:19

17. Strengthening through Obedience

God tells us to love Him with our strength (Mark 12:30) by doing His will with our energy and our bodies (John 14:15). Excuses like "I'm too tired" or "I don't feel like it" don't go over well with the Lord. He gives us strength and He expects us to use it for His glory.

The Bible teaches us a very important principle: obeying God actuates strength. If you are in God's will and obeying God's commands, He will give you the strength you need in every situation Of course you'll still tire, but if you keep trying, God will provide strength through other people or means. For example, when God was leading the Israelites out of Egypt, He told them that obeying His commands would give them the strength to take over the Promised Land (Deut.11:8).

In Exodus 17:8-16, Moses ordered Joshua to pick a few good men and to go fight the Amalekites; then, with God's strength, he was able to help Joshua. In this case, the source of God's strength came through the hands of Moses. When Moses held up his hands, Joshua and his men were winning, but when he lowered them, the Amalekites were winning. Moses held his hands up for a long time until he grew tired, and then Aaron and Hur took over; each took a hand of Moses and held it up until Joshua and his men won. God provided the strength for Joshua and his men to win the fight through Moses, Aaron, and Hur. Though the source of God's strength was Moses' hands, Aaron and Hur kept that source open when Moses was too weary.

In the same way, God uses us to help each other keep the source of His strength wideopen. He uses us to encourage our fellow classmates to keep going when they are too tired to go on. He uses us to help people defend themselves when they are threatened or attacked. We help people everyday in the little things that we do and other people help us, too. "Therefore encourage one another and build each other up, just as in fact you are doing" (1 Thess. 5:11, NIV).

PRINCIPLE	Strength comes from many sources and is actuated by obedience to God.
CODES	1 Corinthians 1:8
	1 Corinthians 15:58
	Ephesians 6:10

18. The Source of our Strength

We use our strength to do amazing things in the martial arts (break boards, throw opponents, etc.). Such abilities come from God and demonstrate His power and might.

Samson was a man of God with great physical and mental strength. He killed a lion with his bare hands (Judg. 14:6) and struck down 1000 Philistine giants with a jawbone (Judg. 15:13-17). The source of his strength came from God by way of his hair; however, a woman was tempted by a large payoff from the Philistines and stole the source from him. When Delilah cut off Samson's hair, she cut off the main source of

Samson's strength through God, and handed him over to the Philistines (Judg. 16:1-22).

While our strength comes from God, it's provided through a source. Today, this source is Jesus Christ. Be careful that nobody cuts off the source of your strength from God, like Delilah did with Samson. People and life, in general, can be very demanding, but you must not allow anyone or anything to keep you from Jesus. Fellowship, prayer, and time spent in the Word of God are critical to maintain a relationship with the Lord. Through Christ we receive strength from God. Without Him, we drown in our own weaknesses.

PRINCIPLE   Strength comes from God through Christ.

CODES   Philippians 4:13
             Ephesians 1:19-20
             Hebrews 11:32-34

19. The Mind of Christ

One of the first tactics that criminals use is manipulation; they try to get into the minds of their potential victims before they actually commit any crime(s). Some do this by creating a situation of fear. They point guns at their victims, they speak loudly and uncaringly, and they threaten to hurt or kill. However, some try to manipulate their potential victims with kindness. Can I help you change that tire on your car? If you get into my car, I'll drive you home. Come with me and I'll help you find your mom or dad. Martial arts training should give us the knowledge and skills to better identify criminals and not fall into their traps.

There are many forces fighting for our minds (Rom. 7:23-25, 8:6; Gal. 4:9). However, as Christian martial artists, we should be single-minded and united in our devotion to God, insusceptible to outside manipulation or trickery (Acts 4:32, 1 Cor. 1:10, James 1:6, 1 Pet. 3:8, 1 John 1:6). We should have the mind of Christ (1 Cor. 2:16, Phil. 2:5). How? Bible Study. The Bible (BKA The Word of God) is the health food for our minds. Without it, our minds are forced to absorb junk in order to survive. Sometimes I get in these lazy streaks and don't like to cook. Since my body still has to eat, I end up eating junk food, fast food, and frozen dinners with very little nutritional value and plenty of harmful chemicals. When I fall into these lazy eating habits, my heath suffers.

Just as the body needs food to survive, the mind does also. In the same way I got lazy with my body (not cooking and eating right), I also got lazy with my mind. When laziness took over, I found myself not studying the Word of God, and instead, absorbing the junk around me from shows on television, stories in the newspaper, trash on the Internet, the unbelief of other people, the political views of the community, etc. This junk caused me to forget God's perfect law, which sets us free. I started to believe all the lies around me and before I knew it, I was changing, not feeling good, not feeling complete, and missing all that God had wanted and prepared for me on earth. However, God would usually bop me on the head repeatedly and wake me up.

We must feed our minds with God's Word in order to be healthy and strong in Him and His Way. If we don't, then our minds will be hungry and find something else to eat. Through healthy mental food and the work of the Holy Spirit, God transforms our minds to be like Christ (Rom. 12:2). The Spirit of the Lord works in us and we become increasingly like Him (2 Cor. 3:18).

PRINCIPLE   The Word of God is health food for the mind.

CODES   Romans 12:2
             2 Corinthians 13:11
             Jeremiah 17:10

20. Attitude Adjustment

What is an attitude? An attitude is the way in which we look at things. We all have one, and we all need to adjust it from time to time. Some folks like to refer to our attitude as either positive or negative, but it's a lot more complicated than that. Seeing a glass as halfway full or halfway empty is relevant only according to the purpose of the contents. After all, seeing a glass halfway full of water, rather than halfway empty, is good if the water is for drinking. It isn't so good if it's for spilling on someone's homework. On the other hand, seeing a glass halfway full of diarrhea, rather than halfway empty, is good if the diarrhea is for fertilizing crops, but not so good if someone accidentally drinks it, thinking it's chocolate milk. Anyway, you get the idea; a so-called positive attitude isn't really positive if the contents of that attitude are not in line with God's purpose.

As a young martial artist, I was taught never to say the word "can't" because supposedly I "could" do anything I set my mind to do. While the rule was understandable, it wasn't very realistic in a larger sense. Sure, I could do 50 pushups if I used every last ounce of energy and sweat in my body, but I couldn't fly with my arms extended like wings. Let's face it, there are many things we can do, but not everything. The Bible tells us that we can do all things through Jesus Christ and through the laws that God established (including natural laws like the law of gravity), not through our own free will. It's according to God's will whether or not He gives us ability and power beyond natural laws. Sometimes He allows miracles, and sometimes He doesn't; anyway you look at it, we can only do what God gives us the power and ability to do. So, we shouldn't make ourselves out to be superheroes, but rather, servants of the only superhero that we know... Jesus Christ.

The Bible tells us to seek God's kingdom and righteousness (Matt. 6:33), to fix our eyes on what is unseen, and not on what is seen (2 Cor. 4:18). Our attitude should be the same as Christ's (Phil. 2:5). "Finally, brothers, whatever is true, whatever is noble, whatever is right, whatever is pure, whatever is lovely, whatever is admirable—if anything is excellent or praiseworthy—think about such things" (Phil. 4:8, NIV). This type of wholesome thinking only comes from the Word of God (2 Pet. 3:1); it cannot be attained through any other means. If you read the Word and allow it to change you, then you know that a positive attitude is not about training the mind as much as it's about changing the heart. All attitude adjustments are done through the Word of God that gets into hearts and changes minds. Attitude adjustments are very important, but they must be done through God. God decided a long time ago what is positive and what is negative, all we need to do is hear and believe.

PRINCIPLE   Our attitude should line up with the Word. If it doesn't, it needs a check.

CODES   2 Corinthians 4:18
             Philippians 2:5
             2 Peter 3:1

21. Focus

The ability to focus is important for martial arts and life. Without it, we are blown to and fro in the wind, having no direction, no purpose, and no victory. People without the ability to focus usually drop out of martial arts or other commitments early on and don't do very much with their lives. They are aimless wanderers; instead of taking hold of the future, they let the future take hold of them. They may drift from one religion to another, get caught up in drugs and alcohol, and frequently change jobs. They are usually unable to commit to people and relationships and they cause burden and strife in other people's lives because they don't know how to take care of themselves.

Being a martial artist requires a lot of focus. Think about it; to spar in a ring requires focus on a few of your own techniques, focus on an opponent's techniques, and focus on the surrounding environment (the ring). To break a board also requires focus on your technique, on speed/power, and on a point beyond a target. If you've ever tried to spar in ring or break a board without proper focus, then you probably know how it hurts. Being a Christian requires a lot of focus, too. It requires focus on Biblical principles and on your one and only Savior and Master, the Lord Jesus Christ. It also requires focus on your surrounding environment and what you allow into your eyes, ears, and mind.

As children, parents, brothers, sisters, spouses, friends, colleagues, consultants, customers, and martial artists we must learn how to focus. We must learn how to bring our minds, bodies, and souls under submission to Christ and His will. Being a Christian is not about us, it's about Christ, and it's about the Father. Let us remember our role is self-sacrifice, an ongoing process and never-ending battle against spiritual forces that want us to believe and do just the opposite. Christian martial artists use the focus that comes from martial arts training to clarify and sharpen their walk with Christ. They know that what they focus on and how they focus reflects who they are as martial artists and as Christians. They know that they were put on earth for a purpose and that God designed them to focus on and complete that purpose.

PRINCIPLE	It's necessary to focus in order to see things clearly, but also to be victorious in martial arts and life according to the Christian way.
CODES	Colossians 3:2
	1 Peter 4:7

22. Achieving Our Goals

In martial arts, we are expected to be goal-oriented from the time we walk in the door and begin classes. Our first goal is yellow belt, our next is orange, and so it continues as long as we continue in martial arts. We know that black belt is a very hard goal to reach, but we diligently work toward it. From the time we accept Christ as our Lord and Savior, we are also expected to be goal-oriented. Our lives are for God and His purposes, not for us and ours. God gives us the tools and sets us up to achieve; we just have to learn what the tools are and how to use them. Once we do, God gradually transforms us into the men and women that He wants us to be, under and for His purposes in heaven.

To reach a goal, we must set out on a journey. To set out on a journey, we must take a step. To take a step, we must have a goal in mind. Life is a series of journeys that take us to a series of goals. From the time we are born, we are already journeying to reach goals, well before we even know what a goal is. In the first two years of life, we learn to scoot, roll over, crawl, sit, walk, talk, eat, drink, run, jump, and the list goes on for pages. Once we get hold of the basics, we learn to read, write, add, subtract, multiply, divide, and the list goes on for pages. As we become adults, our journeys seem to diversify, but our goals are very much the same (family, friends, career, spiritual growth/maturity). And so is our Christian walk; individual journeys are different but the goal is the same.

As Christians, our journey is unity and maturity in the faith and knowledge of Jesus Christ (Eph. 4:13). Our goal is the salvation of our souls (1 Pet. 1:9). The individual goals we strive to achieve everyday only amount to one big goal that God set before us. God put us on earth to be filtered of the evil that exists in our hearts, and to be refined and prepared for eternity, from our own free will. It's our choice if we want our life to be used for that which it was created. It's our choice whether or not to be filtered of evil, refined, and prepared. If we don't meet the goal, then we cease to exist; our souls are burned, consumed, and destroyed by the fire of sin and death. Like a pot is formed from a ball of clay, or a diamond from a speck of dust, so is a life that is given over to its creator.

Think about it...if we weren't meant to achieve, then we wouldn't be given a chance to be born, to grow up, and to grow old. We wouldn't be given a setup called life on earth, only to die and leave it all behind. God created life with a goal in mind, and Satan created another. Therefore, make sure you have your eyes on the right goal! It would be a waste for you to get to the end of this journey called life, only to find you've been journeying towards the wrong goal. Satan wants you to be on his team. He wants you to fight and score points for him so that he can get even with God for kicking him out of heaven and not letting him do what he wanted. Satan doesn't care about the consequences of your soul; all Satan cares about is revenge. Don't be a fool; God loves you.

PRINCIPLE	All your individual goals should add up to one big goal—the salvation of souls in the Lord Jesus Christ.
CODES	1 Corinthians 9:24-27
	Philippians 3:14
	Colossians 2:18

23. Keeping your Head

The judges called me to the ring. My opponent was larger than I and looked really tough, so I smiled at her to break the ice and set a tone of sportsmanship between us. Instead of smiling back, she glared at me and snarled, as if she was going to kick the smile right off my face. Then she looked me in the eye and called me a loser! Suddenly, I felt a rush of anger and insecurity surge through my veins. How could this woman call me a loser? Did I look scrawny and weak? I had had several strategies and plans to overcome larger and tougher opponents, but it all seemed to fly out the window when my focus turned inward to my own emotions and me.

Consequently, I went into the ring feeling angry and intimidated. Everything that I had practiced in preparation for the tournament was suddenly gone, as if I had left it on the sidelines with my stuff. All I could think about was how this mean woman offended me and how I had to beat her no matter what. I lost confidence in my strategies and began to charge her with outright brutality and strength. I wanted to show her that I wasn't scrawny and weak and that I could knock her around. I should have known better; part of her strategy was to make me angry so that I wouldn't fight well. Instead of showing her, I lost the match three to zero because she outsmarted me with strategy and skill.

The point of this story is to demonstrate my failure in this particular tournament from a Christian worldview and life perspective. I let my opponent get to me and temporarily lost my head. I could have beaten her. I was quicker and had good strategy, but I let my emotions take control of my mind. In addition, I reacted as if I had something to prove rather than a fight to win. Satan and his legion of demons try to do the same thing in our Christian lives; they try to trip us up by making us feel angry or insecure, intimidated by them and their counterparts. Satan wants us to believe that we have something to prove, rather than a fight to win. He wants us to be consumed with ourselves so that we are not consumed with doing God's will and reaching out to others.
As Christians, we need to be mindful of how we react to other people and things in the world. When someone says something rude or offensive, it's easy to lose our heads and forget everything we ever learned in the Bible. Before we lose our

heads, we should stop and pray, refocus on the Lord before the moment blurs things so much that we cannot see. The Bible is full of strategies, and the biggest and most important is Jesus Christ. Through Christ, we can keep our heads and overcome all things. Through Christ comes love and confidence, which enables us to win all battles in the Christian way of life. All we have to do is stay focused on Him and not get distracted by our emotions or ourselves.

PRINCIPLE   Keep your head and your strategy in Christ.

CODES   James 1:19-20
                    2 Timothy 4:5
                    2 Corinthians 3:4

24. Moving Meditation and Prayer

We do two things at the beginning of every martial arts class: pray and meditate. When we pray, we talk to God. We ask Him questions, we tell Him things, and we invite Him to work out with us and teach us new things through it. When we meditate, we sit down, relax, and listen to God as He speaks to us. We do this by taking time out and spending it with Him. He wants to spend good, quality time with us every day of our lives.

Have you ever tried to have a relationship with someone whom you never spend time? Have you ever tried to talk to someone who can't seem to sit still and listen? When I'm sharing my heart with a friend, I expect her to listen to me. If I sense that she isn't listening, then I stop sharing and move to lighter topic like work, school, or the weather. Well, God does the same thing with us; if we aren't listening, He doesn't bother.

As Christian martial arts students, we are learning how to fight with our bodies and minds against spiritual forces of evil. Our power comes from God. Prayer and meditation is the communication pathway we use to access God, His Kingdom, and His Power. If we shut down those communication lines, then we shut down the power and strength that comes from Him. Keeping the lines of communication open is challenging, but necessary.

Consequently, we must always pray and meditate, even when we are going about our busy day-to-day lives. Those who practice tai chi really practice moving meditation. The thought is it promotes the circulation of life energy within the body, which brings health and vitality to life. In China, people get up very early to practice the movements before beginning their day; it's just as important as that morning coffee or tea for many.

Kata (forms) can also be practiced as a moving meditation/prayer time. This type of practice can teach us how to spend good quality time with God, and how to listen to and pray to God on all occasions. It can teach us how to keep the communication lines open even when we are doing other things, like washing dishes, preparing dinner, etc. The Bible tells us to practice moving meditation and prayer. Check out the codes below.

PRINCIPLE   Moving meditation and prayer is listening and talking to God at all times, knowing that He is with us every moment of our lives.

CODES   Ephesians 6:18
                    Luke 18:1
                    Psalm 119:97

25. Meditation

Meditation has always played a pivotal role in martial arts training; good meditation skills usually precede good martial arts skills. As contrary as they may seem, the two go hand in hand. Martial artists meditate in order to prepare for combat. They know that serenity and relaxation beget speed and power, and/or redirecting speed and power.

The martial arts and Christianity have one thing in common: their wisdom is found in paradoxes. Think about it. In the martial arts, we have yin/yang, soft/hard, yield/strike, relaxation/speed, and open/closed. In Christianity, we know that God chose the weak to be strong, the last to be first, leaders to be a servants, and death to bring life.

Many things that seem to be quite the opposite are actually quite complementary. That's the way God designed them. It takes relaxed muscles to create power. It takes death of the sinful self in order to experience life in the Spirit. It takes great servitude to make great leadership and a good man to make a good woman (and vice versa).

Applied wisdom, my friend, is learning the meaning of *complementary*. If you want to be a good martial artist, then you have to learn how to meditate and relax. If you want to be a good Christian, then you have to learn how to meditate and allow the Lord to speak and work in your life. A restful sleep comes from a productive day and a productive day comes from a restful sleep. One cannot exist without the other.

PRINCIPLE	Meditation complements martial arts and Christianity like sleeping complements life.
CODES	Joshua 1:8
	Psalm 48:9
	Psalm 119:27
	Psalm 119:48

26. Soul and Spirit

While the nature of man is more commonly viewed as a tri-existence of body, soul, and spirit, Jesus does not teach us to love God with our spirits. This is because spirits are not made to love, but to connect people's bodies, minds, and souls to God. While the soul makes a human being into a unique individual, the spirit gives a human being life through God. In more simple terms, the soul is the personal and the spirit is the transpersonal part of our making. The same way that an umbilical cord connects a fetus to its life-giving source, a spirit supernaturally connects a soul to its maker, God.

While the human spirit was created by God and continues to bring physical life to the body until God deems otherwise, it's incapable of connecting our minds and souls to God. This is because we have all sinned (Rom. 3:23), and sin separates us from God (Isa. 59:2) and kills us (Rom. 6:23, 8:13). If we want to be connected to God, and to have eternal life through Him, then we have no other choice but to give ourselves over to and be born again through Jesus Christ, allowing Him to save us from sin and death (Rom. 6:23, 8:2; I John 5:11-13).

Jesus is the Messiah (John 4:26) and one with God (John 10:30); He is the truth, the way, and the life, and the only path to the Father (John 14:6). If we are born again through Jesus Christ, we receive a new Spirit from the Lord, one that is capable of fully connecting us to Him. This new Spirit brings our entire beings (bodies, minds, and souls) into a new personal relationship with the Father, saves us from our transgressions, and assures us eternal life. It totally renews our bodies, minds, and souls. All we have to do is believe in Jesus and receive Him in our lives (John 1:12).

PRINCIPLE	The Spirit is the connection between God and us; the soul is the precious gift that the Lord has saved through Christ. Both are made from the same essence: God.
CODES	Hebrews 4:12
	Ezekiel 18:24
	Matthew 10:28

27. Living in the Spirit

After becoming a Christian, the Bible teaches to "Watch ye and pray, lest ye enter into temptation: The spirit truly is ready, but the flesh is weak" (Mark 14:38, KJV). This weakness is constantly tested by a quick and easy society that caters to the desires of the flesh, to sin. Sin is everything that is contrary to the Bible; it's not just disobedience to the Ten Commandments. Thus, no matter how hard one tries, it's impossible to stop sinning without the Spirit of life in Jesus Christ. "This I say then, Walk in the Spirit, and ye shall not fulfill the lust of the flesh. For the flesh lusteth against the Spirit, and the Spirit against the flesh: and these are contrary the one to the other: so that ye cannot do the things that ye would" (Gal. 5:16-17, KJV).

When the flesh rules the life of someone, the body, mind, and soul are saturated with self and death. However, when the Spirit rules the life of someone (after personally accepting Jesus Christ as Lord and Savior), the body, mind, and soul are permeated with love and life. Since God is love, and human beings are incapable of loving without Him (1 John 4:8), the Spirit must reside in all those who love. Only when people accept Jesus Christ as Lord and Savior, and connect to God through the Spirit, will they learn how to truly love Him with their bodies, minds, and souls and surrender their lives to His will. In Romans 12, Paul urges his followers to do just this, to offer themselves as living sacrifices and renew themselves unto the Lord.

As a human being, Jesus went through vigorous hardship to discipline His body, mind, and soul, submit His entire being to the Father; and prepare himself for ministry. Following His baptism by John, He was led into the wilderness on foot and then stayed there alone for forty days and nights with no food (Matt. 4). He resisted the longing of the flesh to eat, and He refused to give in to the various temptations of the devil. "No discipline is enjoyable while it is happening—it is painful! But afterward there will be a quiet harvest of right living for those who are trained in this way" (Heb. 12:11, NLT). While the spiritual battle was far from easy, Jesus was more than victorious in the end; He saved all of our souls from the fire of hell.

Christians fight a spiritual battle in life much like Jesus fought in the wilderness. They typically do not travel to a physical wilderness for long periods, without food or water, to have a face-to-face confrontation with Satan. Nonetheless, they endure every day trials, temptations, and sometimes, lengthy tribulations by producing the Fruit of the Spirit (Gal. 5:22-23) and using the only infallible form of self-defense on Earth, the full Armor of God (Eph. 6:10-18). Through Christ, these are the only tools that give Christians victory over temptation and protection from Satan's tricks and schemes.

PRINCIPLE	Live in the Spirit, not in the flesh.
CODES	Matthew 26:41
	Mark 1:8
	Luke 1:35
	John 6:63

28. Rituals

A ritual is a customarily repeated and formal act or series of acts. We have all sorts of rituals in our lives. Getting up in the morning and brushing our teeth is a ritual. Driving to work or taking the bus to school is a ritual. In martial arts class, we also have rituals. Putting on our uniforms and tying our belts is a ritual. Bowing in and out of class is a ritual, too. Rituals make up our daily lives, and no matter how hard we try, we cannot escape them.

Accept it... rituals are a part of life and they exist for a reason. However, when we do the same thing repeatedly, it's easy to forget why. It has been my experience that when people forget the reason why they do the same thing again and again, their once-upon-a-time rituals turn into routines and traditions. A routine is a ritual without a living purpose and a tradition is a ritual whose purpose was lost in the family somewhere along the line.

The Bible tells us to practice certain rituals. A perfect example is communion. We take communion to consciously acknowledge and accept Christ as our personal savior because of what He did for us. However, when we forget the reason why we take it, it loses its intrinsic value and becomes mere routine. Instead of taking communion with a true sense of repentance and willingness to be a living sacrifice for Christ, our Savior, we simply go through the motions. We take it because we were taught to take it and it's right.

Like communion, God uses us to change our routines and traditions into rituals that involve Him in the purpose. When we get up in the morning and brush our teeth, it's to serve the

Lord. When we go to a job or school that we don't necessarily enjoy, we do it for God, not just a paycheck. When we
put on our uniforms and belts and bow in and out of class,
practice our techniques, or use martial arts on the street, it's
for God and His glory, not our own. The key to the Christian
life, is transforming lifeless routines and traditions in
purposeful rituals that serve the Creator and His ways.

PRINCIPLE   Our rituals should have a purpose.

CODES   1 Corinthians 10:31
             1 Corinthians 11:23-26
             John 6:27

29. Worship

What is worship? It isn't going to church on Sunday and then
living in sin for the rest of the week. Worship is offering our
bodies as living sacrifices to God (Rom. 12:1), all the time.
While people like to separate the two, the body and spirit and
intricately connected. Like the yin/yang, the body and spirit
work together harmoniously to worship. The Bible tells us
that what is sown in a natural body is raised up into a spiritual
one (1 Cor. 15:44); therefore, everything we do with our
natural body (and mind) has spiritual significance and effects.
We are here for one purpose. Don't be mistaken by thinking
you can do some things outside of your religious beliefs and
be okay with God. You can't!

Knowing the true purpose of life, we have to work together to
unify our churches and ourselves in this regard. The first
thing we have to do is understand that everything in our lives

has spiritual significance and purpose, whether we recognize it or not. Going to the store, cooking dinner, doing homework, working on a project, hanging out with friends, and practicing martial arts all have spiritual significance and purpose; they either glorify you (and subsequently Satan) or they glorify God. I received an email from a person the other day; it read as follows:

> *As a Christian and a third Dan Instructor, I think you are greatly mistaken to join the two. It's wrong to mix Christianity with Taoist and Buddhist philosophy. Jesus does not help us perform martial arts and he does not ask it of us. He cannot be our Master in this regard.*

This man claims to be a Christian and a martial arts instructor, but is unable to mix the two. The Bible is very clear about the things that we do with our bodies (and minds) on earth; "Whatever you eat or drink or whatever you do, you must do all for the glory of God" (1 Cor. 10:31, NLT). I hope this man is reading the same Bible that I read; it's clear as crystal—if you can't mix it, then you shouldn't do it. We cannot be divided as Christians; we are either living sacrifices or we are not. We either bring glory to God by what we do or we do not. It really isn't that difficult to understand; everything we do—our whole lives—should be devoted to God's work and purpose in some shape or form.

PRINCIPLE	Give yourself fully to the work of the Lord, as a living sacrifice.
CODES	Romans 12:1-2; 1 Corinthians 15:44
	John 4:25; 1 Peter 2:4-5
	Philippians 2:1-2

SPIRITUAL

PHYSICAL   MENTAL

Chapter 7

Loving My Neighbors As Myself

The second is equally important:
'Love your neighbor as yourself.'
No other commandment
is greater than these.

~ Mark 12: 31, NLT

30. To Love: The Greatest Commandment

When the Pharisees questioned Jesus about the greatest commandment, Jesus replied it's to love the Lord God with all your heart, soul, strength, and mind. In the same teaching, Jesus outlined the second greatest commandment, which is to love your neighbors as much as you love yourself. This teaching can be found in Matthew 22:34-40, Mark 12:28-34, and Luke 10:25-28, and emphasizes the total-person involvement in love.

While the greatest commandment is really about God and us, the second greatest commandment involves other people. The word "neighbors" in the Bible does not refer to people who live on our block, it refers to all people with whom we meet throughout the course of our lives, including our enemies (Matt. 5:44). So, in essence, God wants us (1) to love Him with our entire beings and (2) to love others and ourselves alike.

And so we get to the benefits of Christian martial arts: a tool for mental, physical, spiritual, and social training in love. Love is not feeling; it's decision and action. It's very important to thoroughly understand the command "to love" and apply it to your training and life. True understanding and application will not only improve your martial arts skills, techniques, and strategies; it will help you to lead a purposeful and fulfilling life in the Lord Jesus Christ.

PRINCIPLE Use the teaching, understanding, and application of the greatest and second greatest commandments to enhance your martial arts training and life.

CODES   Matthew 22:40
              1 Thessalonians 3:12
              Romans 13:10

31. The Strategy of Patience

Loving ourselves and other people means being patient. Patience is not only an attribute of love; it's a facet of the Fruit of the Spirit. This means it comes from salvation through Jesus Christ. Two scriptures in the Bible very clearly demonstrate patience, from the viewpoint of martial arts:

- "A hot-tempered man stirs up dissension, but a patient man clams a quarrel" (Prov. 15:18, NIV).
- "Better a patient man than a warrior, a man who controls his temper than one who takes a city" (Prov. 16:32, NIV).

What does this mean in terms of how we love? It means not losing our tempers or giving up. Patience is not only a sign of love, but also an expression of wisdom (Prov. 19:11) and a tool of persuasion (Prov. 25:15); it's a strategy for winning before a fight ever begins. In cases where fighting is unavoidable, patience is still at work. God had enormous patience with us; he gave us covenant after covenant for 1000 years before sending Jesus Christ, and then He gave us unlimited patience thereafter (1 Tim. 1:16). True patience means "salvation" (2 Pet. 3:15) and inherits God's promises (Heb. 6:12).

While patience will keep us from starting or escalating battles, it will not keep us from fighting. Evil does not stop because we patiently wait for it to stop and God calls us to stand up and fight against it from time to time. On the battlefield, patience is displayed by the way in which we fight, by using the appropriate amount of force to escape and get to a safe place. Impatience (especially in the form of anger or rage) is evident by excessive force, which often leads to unnecessary injury or death. There are many ways to thwart an attack; the goal of every Christian martial artist is to use patience as a value and strategy to prevent battles and/or excessive force when a battle is unavoidable.

The Bible teaches us to forgive evil acts but not to excuse them. If a man rapes someone who we know and love, then God asks us to forgive him and pray for him. If a man tries to rape someone who we know and love, then God asks us to stand against his act and intervene, if we are in a position to do so. When we fight, we should remember that we are combating evil acts and not hopelessly evil people. If God had His way, all people would come to live in his right-eousness and goodness. We should pray for even those people who have committed the most hideous crimes, and hope that they repent and follow Jesus. So, as Christian martial artists, let us be slow to destroy and quick to forgive (from safe ground).

PRINCIPLE   Patience is wise and prudent strategy.

CODES   Proverbs 14:29
             Proverbs 19:11
             Proverbs 25:15

32. Kill with Kindness

Loving ourselves and other people means being kind. Kindness is not only an attribute of love; it's a facet of the Fruit of the Spirit. This means it comes from salvation through Jesus Christ. Two scriptures in the Bible very clearly demonstrate kindness, from the martial arts perspective:

- "A kind man benefits himself, but a cruel man brings trouble on himself" (Prov. 11:17, NIV).
- "Make sure that nobody pays back wrong for wrong, but always be kind to each other and to everyone else" (1 Thess. 5:15, NIV).

Notice the wisdom of the Bible; a kind man benefits HIMSELF. Obvious are the benefits for the recipients of kindness; not so obvious are the benefits for the providers. People who are unkind generally believe that being kind will hurt or deter them in some way. Being nice to someone whom your friends dislike may make you look bad and disliked, too. Going out of your way to help an elder to cross the street may make you late for a meeting.

While the world would like you to think otherwise, the "you" perspective is usually more beneficial than the "me" perspective. Let's say you took the risk and were nice to someone whom your so-called friends disliked. Your so-called friends may outwardly appear to dislike you but secretly admire you for taking a stand. You may also gain a much better and closer friend than you've ever had before. Who knows what can come of helping an elder to cross the street? The benefits can be pleasantly surprising.

As Christian martial artists, we should go against the norm to be kind and our skills should never be used in any way to avenge. Kindness has a way of killing strife and planting seeds of peace where they never grew before. Paying back wrong for wrong is not kind; it's rooted in anger and bitterness, which the Bible teaches to get rid of in our lives (Eph. 4:31). If we are focusing our time and energy on avenging ourselves, then we cannot be focusing on God's will and work on earth. Our lives are worth nothing unless we use them to do work assigned to us by the Lord Jesus Christ, to share Good News about God's love and kindness (Acts 20:24).

God never asks us to do anything that He doesn't do, Himself. In His great patience, God showed us great kindness by sending His Son Jesus Christ to save us (Eph. 2:7). God asks us to be kind to others so that He can reach them with His love; "I led them with cords of human kindness, with ties of love; I lifted the yoke from their neck and bent down to feed them" (Hos. 11:4, NIV). Kindness should always be our attitude and first line of defense.

PRINCIPLE   Kill with kindness before force.

CODES   2 Corinthians 6:1
             Ephesians 1:6
             Ephesians 4:32

33. Love is not Jealous

Love is not jealous (1 Cor. 13:4), but God is a jealous God (Ex. 20:5). While these two statements seem to contradict each other, they really don't. God is jealous "for" us, not "of" us. He doesn't envy who we are or what we have; He is saddened about what we don't have. "I am jealous for you with a godly jealously...but I am afraid that just as Eve was deceived by the serpent's cunning, your minds may somehow be led astray from your sincere and pure devotion to Christ" (2 Cor. 11:2-3, NIV).

In much the same way, we are not jealous of our kids; we don't envy after and desire for ourselves the things that they are and have. We are jealous for our kids; we want their love and devotion because we birthed them, raised them, and know what is best for their health and well-being. We want to enjoy them in the love through which God created our children, and we want them to enjoy us. We don't want them rebelling against the love that we have for them, or calling someone else "mother" or "father" when we are their rightful parents. In this way, we are made in the image of God, to love and be loved.

As Christian martial artists, we should not envy (1 Pet. 2:1 NIV), or be jealous in the worldly sense of the word. Envy is another product of the "me" perspective that leads us into ourselves instead of God and His will. It's misleading in that the person who envies thinks that someone else has it better than they do. If they only had a bigger house, a better job, and more money like Bob, then they'd be happy. Not so—envy, even fulfilled, leaves us just as empty, if not more so, than we were before we received what we envied after. Envy is not the answer to our problems; it's a distraction from our life and its purpose.

It's easy to envy martial arts champions and stars, and they often want you to envy them. This is what opens the door to manipulation and misguided spirituality in many secular martial arts schools. So-called masters who do not point the way to Christ set students up to envy them in every sense of the word. Once the students desire and covet what the masters have, then the students have opened a door for the masters to enter into their minds, bodies, and souls. At this juncture, so-called masters can very easily lead the students anywhere in sin and death.

Christian martial artists should avoid envy at all costs. The Bible tells us not to let our hearts envy sinners (Prov. 23:17). There is only one person that we should strive to be like, and that person is Jesus Christ. The only other thing we should strive after is the Kingdom of God; "But seek ye first the kingdom of God, and his righteousness; and all these things shall be added unto you" (Matt. 6:33).

PRINCIPLE   Jealousy and envy leads to sin and death.

CODES   Proverbs 14:30
             Proverbs 24:1
             Proverbs 3:31
             Galatians 5:26

34. Love is not Boastful

Boasting, bragging, going on and on about our undertakings and ourselves is what God wants us to stay away from. It's good to go to tournaments and win, but let's not get too consumed or bigheaded about it. As Christians, we are supposed to demonstrate love in all that we say and do, and love is not boastful.

I once knew a man who just couldn't stop praising himself no matter who he was conversing with or where the conversation would go. Even when other people were being honored, he was trying to steal their spotlight and claim all the attention for himself. He tried to outdo others so much that people just stopped talking to him. They would actually run the other way whenever he came around.

While boasting is typically thought to be something we do about ourselves, it can be focused on other people, too. A mother who goes on and on about all of the tournaments that her son has won, and how many trophies are sitting on his desk, is boasting. Being proud is one thing, but being boastful is another thing altogether. Proud parents praise the Lord Jesus Christ for the good things in their children; boastful parents praise their children.

Loving ourselves means not boasting about ourselves but praising the Lord above who saved us. Loving others means not glorifying them as individuals and losing sight of the role that God plays in their lives. We must be careful about what we teach our children; they are not worthy without the Lord Jesus Christ, and we never want them to think they are. As proud as we can become of our children or friends, we need to show them that we are giving the Lord all the credit. They are simply recipients of the Lords goodness.

PRINCIPLE	Give praise to the Lord for the good things in others; do not boast about them or their accomplishments.
CODES	Ephesians 2:8-9
	1 Corinthians 1:31
	2 Corinthians 10:17-18
	Galatians 6:14

35. Love is not Arrogant

It's well known that martial arts builds confidence in students who train seriously. What is not so well known is that martial arts can also build arrogance when the focus is on self. Confident people are sure of their nature and abilities without comparing themselves to others; arrogant people are sure of their nature and abilities by setting themselves up to be superior to others. Ironically, arrogant people have lower self-esteem than those who are confident; their opinion of themselves is based on their ability to "be better than" and "outdo" everyone around them.

Arrogant people are uninviting and hard to reach, making it difficult for ministry and healing to occur in their lives. Both the church and martial arts have played a role in developing arrogance, particularly in Christians. Not associating with sinners because you are not a sinner and you are better than a sinner is arrogant. Criticizing and judging others, while putting yourself up on a pedestal is also arrogant. How can you say to your brother, 'Let me take the speck out of your eye,' when all the time there is a plank in your own eye? You hypocrite, first take the plank out of your own eye, and then you will see clearly to remove the speck from your brother's eye" (Matt. 7:4-5, NIV).

As Christians, we are confident and sure of our nature and ourselves through Jesus Christ. We know that without Jesus, we are as filthy rags (Isa. 64:6) but with Him, we can do all things (Phil. 4:13) for the glory of God. How else can we win God's battles but with confidence? Salvation brings self-confidence and confidence produces people and works that are worthy before the Lord. God wants to build us up in confidence, not tear us down. If you feel that you are not being built up by your church, you should really consider another. "Timothy, my son, here are my instructions for you, based on the prophetic words spoken about you earlier. May they give you the confidence to fight well in the Lord's battles" (1 Tim. 1:18, NLT).

PRINCIPLE   Be confident, not arrogant.

CODES   Isaiah 2:17
Hebrews 4:16
Philippians 1:6

36. Love is Not Rude

Loving others means doing your best not to be rude. Since rudeness is based on one's perception, it means understanding how other people view your words and behaviors. Most arguments and fights are a result of "perceived" rudeness. Some people know when they are being rude and don't care, but most are unaware that others perceive them as being rude. This can happen a lot when people from different parts of the world encounter each other. In parts of Africa, it's considered rude to cross your legs. In parts of Latin America, it's considered rude to throw something to someone. In parts of Asia, it's considered rude to stand on a chair or put your feet up on a table with your shoes on; and in parts of Europe, it's considered rude to be even a little bit wasteful of electricity or water.

Perceived rudeness can and does often differ across families, too. In some families, belching out loud, walking around the house without shoes on, or using someone else's things without asking is considered to be perfectly normal, whereas other families might consider it to be rude. What some parents allow their kids to do freely at home can be considered rude and obnoxious at someone else's home. Not being rude is more than simply not doing things that you think are rude; it's truly understanding what rude means to different people from different nationalities, ethnicities, cultures, and families. It means looking beyond yourself to understand how others view you and your behavior, and adjusting yourself accordingly. This isn't always easy; it takes a great deal of observation and attentiveness.

It's one thing to know what may be perceived as rude and not do it, but it's something else to go out of your way to do something polite not be perceived as rude. Sometimes we don't do things that we ought and our inaction makes us look rude and ungrateful. For example, someone may give us a gift and we neglect to write a thank-you note because we are so busy. We may forget someone's birthday and neglect to give him/her a card or gift. We may not pay someone back who lent us money, or we may casually forget to return something that another person so generously lent us. There are many things that we don't do that could make us look like uncaring, rude people. Even if thank-you notes and birthday cards aren't important to us, they may be very important to other people.

As a Christian martial artist, you must realize the effect that your attitude and behavior has on other people. You must be willing to go the extra mile, not to be rude, but to be polite. Maybe it means not riding someone's bumper or beeping your horn continuously when someone in front of you is driving too slowly. Maybe it means not walking on a turf that someone else claims to be his, even if you don't think it's his or that it's rude to walk on it. Maybe it means taking someone out for coffee that you know doesn't like you and making the first move toward peace and reconciliation.

Whatever it is for you, not being perceived as rude is a major step in avoiding unnecessary conflict. It's one way that we show love for others and ourselves. We aren't rude to ourselves and those who are like us, but we must be careful not to be rude to those who are different, too.

PRINCIPLE	Be careful about how your words and behaviors are interpreted by other people; love is not perceived as rude.
CODES	Luke 17:2
	Proverbs 18:19
	James 3:2

37. Love is not Selfish

From the day we are born, we learn what is ours and what is not. We develop a sense of ownership towards money, time, people, etc. For some of us, giving our things and ourselves comes naturally, but for others, it's very hard to let go. Nonetheless, love is not selfish. Being selfish means not sharing, and not being selfish means sharing. Sharing is not keeping who we are and what we have to ourselves, but it's not giving all that we are and have to other people, either. Sharing is a 50/50 proposition; God calls us to love others "as" we love ourselves, not more and not less.

I've met very poor people who would give the shirt off their back to help someone in need. I've also met very rich people who wouldn't give a dollar to someone in need. "It is more blessed to give than to receive" (Acts 20:35, KJV), but giving must be done with Godly direction and wisdom. What good would it do to give all your money and possessions to the poor and not have enough to take care of yourself and your family? Well, it would help the poor temporarily, but when the money and possessions were used up and gone, then there would be no more to give. You wouldn't be able to have a job because you wouldn't have what you needed to commit to one (i.e. a car, gasoline, food, a house).

If you give a man a fish, he'll eat for a day; if you teach a man to fish, he'll eat for a lifetime. The wise helper spends more time teaching a man to fish than resources giving him fish, but he does both. He gives his resources and time. Jesus gave essentials of life, but more importantly, He taught people how to live their lives. He took time to give what the Lord told Him to give, and He took time to receive what the

Lord told Him to receive. Jesus didn't spend all of His time and resources teaching and healing people; He spent a lot of time with God and training His disciples to carry on His work when He was gone. Did this make Jesus selfish? No. The time that Jesus spent with God and training His disciples actually helped all people in the end.

Christianity is a lot like martial arts. We cannot teach martial arts without first learning and practicing it repeatedly. Likewise, we cannot give any good gifts to other people, unless we spend a great deal of time receiving good gifts from God. Not being selfish is really about balance…balance between you and the world, giving and taking. We should always keep our glass half-full, not giving away all that we are and have, and not retaining too much of what we are and have either. It's not very wise as a Christian to spend yourself completely or to keep yourself from being spent. Nor is it wise as a martial artist to spend all of your time training and not teaching or all of our time teaching and not training. Love is not selfish, but giving, and God calls us to be giving to ourselves AND to others.

PRINCIPLE   Not being selfish is about balance.

CODES   Romans 12:6-8
            Matthew 5:6
            Luke 6:38

38. Love is not Easily Angered

Love is not easily angered (1 Cor. 13:5 NIV) because it isn't dependent on what other people say or do; it's only dependent on what God says and does. This doesn't mean we walk around as happy as larks, all the time; there is a difference between getting angry and feeling angry. Getting angry is action-oriented and refers to what one says and how one behaves when the feeling of anger arises. Feeling angry is something altogether different that can be brought on by self or God. 1 Corinthians 13:5 is referring to action-oriented anger only. In other translations of the Bible, the scripture says love is "not irritable" (NLT) and "not easily provoked" (KJV), both of which refer to words and behavior.

When Jesus hung on the cross, dying from what other people were saying and doing to him, He probably felt very angry. How could He not? The very people that He wanted to help turned against Him, and even His own disciples betrayed Him…Judas with a kiss and Peter by pretending that he didn't know Jesus, to save his own skin. Nonetheless, as Jesus hung dying alone on the cross, next to thieves, He was careful about how His feelings of anger translated into actions (words and behavior). He said "Father, forgive them; they know not what they do" (Luke 23:34). Note, He didn't say "You idiots, don't you have a clue about what you are doing?" We are allowed to feel angry towards different things, for different reasons. However, rather than respond unkindly, we are to respond in love.

Another thing that Jesus taught us on the cross is that when we are angry, it's better to talk to God about it than to vent at other people. Instead of venting His anger at the people who were persecuting him, Jesus cried out to God, "Father, why have you forsaken me?" (Matt. 27:46). Interestingly enough, that statement implies that Jesus never felt betrayed by people, but rather, abandoned by God. It showed how much

God meant to Jesus and how real and important God was in His life. To Jesus, it didn't matter what people were doing to Him, but what God was doing in the greater scheme of things. The feeling of being abandoned came from His humanness as He reached closer to death in great pain, but hadn't fully comprehended God's plan. Through faith, Jesus finally let go of the feeling of abandonment and committed His spirit into God's hands before He died (Luke 23:46).

Like water quenches fire, love quenches anger. Living water from the heavenly father above can keep our flames of anger under control. When we allow our anger to control us, it produces sin (Jas.1:19-22); however, when we control our anger, it produces righteousness. The Bible isn't instructing us to never feel angry; it's simply telling us to be careful about how we respond when feelings of anger arise. Our words and actions can lead us to life or death. "So also, the tongue is a small thing, but what enormous damage it can do. A tiny spark can set a great forest on fire. And the tongue is a flame of fire. It is full of wickedness that can ruin your whole life. It can turn the entire course of your life into a blazing flame of destruction, for it is set on fire by hell itself" (Jas. 3:5-6, NLT).

PRINCIPLE	Don't allow feelings of anger to lead you into sin, but rather, righteousness.
CODES	Psalm 4:4
	Proverbs 15:1
	Ephesians 4:26-27

39. Love doesn't Keep Records

Love does not keep record of wrongs. In other words, it doesn't allow wrongful acts of the past to turn into criticism and resentment in the future. When we keep a record against ourselves, it's easy to find ourselves in a downward spiral of self-criticism and hatred. When we keep a record against others, resentment builds up inside of us until we're just about to explode. Spiraling downward and/or exploding is not what God wants us to do with our lives; He wants us to serve Him and do His will on earth.

Keeping a record of wrongs is one of Satan's ploys to get us to believe that we are like God and can do all that God does. First, it requires judging people according to a code of conduct, which is only God's role and responsibility. Second, it glorifies self, even in self-criticism and hatred, because it assumes that self is the only source of salvation. Third, it de-Christianizes our minds by focusing only on works and not on the free gift of salvation. Fourth, it distracts us from living our lives out for God and fulfilling His will on earth. From the Garden of Eden to today, Satan's goal is to use you to stop God's work. Be aware!

It's hypocritical and not Christian to judge people based on their failures. In John 8:1-11, the Pharisees brought a woman to Jesus that had been caught in the act of adultery. They asked about stoning her and Jesus replied, "He that is without sin among you, let him first cast a stone at her" (8:7, KJV). All the men were convicted by their own sin and fled. Then, Jesus looked at the woman and said "Woman, where are those thine accusers? hath no man condemned thee?...Neither do I condemn thee: go, and sin no more" (8:10-11, KJV).

No matter what the actions of others, we are called to love them. Christ taught us to love one another as He has loved us (John 13:34-35). Note that Christ did not teach us to hurt and condemn one another as our relatives and friends have hurt and condemned us. As Christian martial artists, we must always be mindful of this truth. We are put on God's earth, in His army, to love and protect His people, not to avenge ourselves against them. When we are called to fight, and sometimes even to kill, the motives must be found in love, not in anger and resentment. Anger and resentment only hurt those who have it (Job 18:4).

PRINCIPLE	Forgive and forget; don't allow records of wrongs to turn into anger, resentment, and hatred.
CODES	Ecclesiastes 7:9
	Job 5:2
	Colossians 3:13

40. Love Rejoices in Truth, not Lies

As human beings, we rejoice in either unrighteousness (lies) or righteousness (truth). Rejoicing in unrighteousness is not jumping for joy over evil; it's believing a lie from Satan and taking pleasure in the actions that encompass the lie. For example, if you believed a lie that you could fly like a bird with nothing but the shirt on your back, then you probably wouldn't hesitate to jump off the side of a mountain, and you would even take pleasure in doing so. You wouldn't see it as a path of death until it was too late, and you had already unknowingly killed yourself in the process. Satan actually tried to get Jesus to believe this lie by sugarcoating it with another lie about God's Word; he called Jesus a chicken and dared Him to jump off the mountain if He really believed God (Luke 4:12). Jesus, of course, didn't fall or jump for Satan.

People rejoice about robbing banks, killing, and cheating, among other things, because they believe in lies like "money will solve all problems," "revenge will bring peace," or "infidelity is okay when there's love." Behind every act of unrighteousness is a lie from the devil. Lies distort and disfigure reality and lead people along the path of death. Some of the biggest lies today are about self, sex, and money, and from the beginning of time, about how we can be like God. The tree of the knowledge of good and evil was the first time that man rejoiced in a lie from Satan, and the first time that man fell. Satan told Eve that she could be like God if she just ate of the fruit of the knowledge of good and evil. He told her that God didn't want her to be like Him, and that His intentions for forbidding the fruit were selfish. He assured her that she would get great pleasure from the fruit, and so she took of it, and ate it. Then she gave some to her husband who also ate it.

As Christian martial artists, it's important to understand that criminal acts are a result of lies, mistaken truth. The criminal mind is one that has been won over by pure lies, and the only way to change it is to fill it with truth. Let's take a serial killer for example; Ted Bundy claimed that he was driven to kill women because of pornography. He believed in pornography and all its lies and took pleasure and rejoiced in using it. Porn taught him that women were objects and that sex was for pure pleasure. These lies led him to commit horrendous acts of unrighteousness. Supposedly, before he was executed, he did learn of the truth and surrendered his life to God. He then rejoiced in revealing the truth to the world about pornography and how its lies produce evil.

PRINCIPLE	Love is the product of believing in and rejoicing in truth.
CODES	Psalm 85:10
	Ephesians 4:15
	John 8:44

41. Love Bears and Protects

To bear something is to be a covering or protection for someone. It involves watching someone's back and looking out for his/her well-being. Bearing all is about protecting others and ourselves in love. As Christian martial artists, this is a very important concept to grasp. Just as police have a job to protect the public under the law, we have a job to protect God-made people under Jesus Christ. Our job is more than physical self-defense; it's mental and spiritual, too. Physical safety doesn't mean much to someone who is mentally and spiritually on a path to death; however, it does buy time for him/her to get on the right path of salvation.

Let's look at a classic example…you encounter a stranger who is trying to harm a child. The first thing you do is protect the child from physical harm by stopping the stranger in his tracks. From a secular point of view, when the child is safe and out of danger, the battle is over and won. However, from a Christian point of view, fighting for physical safety is just the beginning of a war. Yes, the child must be protected from harm, but so must the stranger. While the child needs to be physically protected from a stranger who is influenced by Satan, the stranger needs to be spiritually protected from a murder, liar, and thief named Satan. Obviously, God would have us protect the child first, but let us not forget to pray that the stranger who is lost be found.

Love bears all—which means it protects in every way, shape, and form, not just physically but mentally and spiritually, too. The Bible tells us that husbands are to protect and cover their wives. If a husband just kept his wife from physical harm but abused her mentally and misdirected her spiritually, then he wouldn't be expressing love according to the Bible. How did Christ protect us? His teachings were mental, His miracles were physical, and His death was spiritual. People are not one-dimensional and love is not limited and conditional. If we love in the way in which God tells us to love, then we do what we can to protect all people, even those who inflict harm on others. It's easy to see people as "bad" or "good"; this is a fallacy. According to a Christian worldview, people are either saved or not saved, safe or in danger. When harm is being inflicted, all parties are in danger, in more than one way.

PRINCIPLE	In the Christian worldview, protection is physical, mental, and spiritual.
CODES	Psalm 40:11
	Psalm 97:10
	Proverbs 4:6
	Proverbs 20:28

42. Love Trusts and Believes

As Christians, our job is to trust people through faith in God, even though they may not deserve it. In doing so, we are fulfilling God's will in our lives. Trust is the foundation of all intimacy. Those who are afraid of being hurt by others or God cannot be intimate, and they miss the beauty of relationships and love. Jesus knew in His heart that Judas was going to betray Him for bribe money; however, He still trusted Judas because of their close and loving relationship. Because of that trust, God's will was done on earth, and eventually Judas was condemned by his own heart, returned the bribe money to the chief priests and elders, and hanged himself because he felt so bad (Matt. 27:3-5). When someone trusts you through Jesus Christ, and you break that trust, the Holy Spirit convicts you harshly. To betray someone's trust is much worse than betraying someone who didn't trust you in the first place.

If your best friend betrays you, then God simply asks you to forgive her and entrust her to Him. It doesn't mean that you go on as if nothing happened; it doesn't even mean that you continue the relationship as it was before; it means that you have a positive outlook about who she can become in relationship to you and you don't "assume" that she is going to betray you again if she apologized and asked for forgiveness. God doesn't promise that we won't be hurt; He calls us to trust other people, not as they are, but as God sees them through His faithful love. To love people is to rely on God's trust, knowing that nobody is perfect and people are bound to sin. No matter if others hurt us or not, God will pick us up and comfort us as we heal. Vulnerability brings pain, yes, but it also brings great joy. Pain is a part of being human, and while not many people like to hear it, it's how we learn and grow in faith.

If Jesus had not trusted people through God, then He never would have done what He did. He trusted that God would bring meaning and value into the lives of others through His relationships. His whole ministry was delivered through His relationships. As Christian martial artists, we must be willing to trust people, not through our hearts, but through the heart of God. While trust has a positive outlook, it's not stupid either. Clearly, we shouldn't get into cars with strangers or jog alone at night with a Walkman, trusting that nobody will harm us. Clearly, women shouldn't continue to stay with men who physically abuse them and their children repeatedly, trusting that they won't do it again. Clearly, we must teach children to be careful about whom they trust. In most dictionaries, there are at least two definitions of trust: (1) reliance and confidence in someone or something and (2) hope.

While the Bible tells us to trust, it also tells us not to trust people without reason; "Do not trust a neighbor; put no confidence in a friend" (Mic. 7:5, NIV); "Beware of your friends; do not trust your brothers. For every brother is a deceiver, and every friend a slanderer" (Jer. 9:4, NIV). It says you should only trust those who have proven themselves trustworthy (1 Cor. 4:2). In reference to strangers or people who have proven themselves untrustworthy, trust means hope. In reference to loved ones who have not proven themselves untrustworthy, trust means reliance and confidence. For loved ones who have broken our trust, it means faith vision from near or afar, depending on the status of the relationship. Sometimes relationships can go on and sometimes they must end, but even so, trust has a positive outlook about the person(s) involved. For people we don't know, or to whom we are not relating, trust is displayed in the form of hope and prayer that God's will be done in their lives. It believes in the Lord Jesus Christ to deliver people from evil and unrighteousness.

PRINCIPLE   Trust in God and trust in people through God.

CODES   John 12:36
             John 14:1
             Isaiah 26:4

43. Love Always Hopes

Hope is a positive attitude, in the Christian sense of the word. It's also a caring attitude, wishing and praying the best for everyone. We hope that our children will have more in life than we did. We hope that our brothers and sisters will lead fulfilling and fruitful lives. There is a fine-line difference between trust and hope. Trust is the foundation of our intimacy in relationships and our comfort in the world; hope is praying the best for others, independent of us.

To trust my husband means I can rely on, confide in, or hope for him in relationship to me. I trust my husband will continue working to pay the bills (reliance), to be faithful to me no matter what temptations come his way (confidence), and to rise up to be the spiritual leader of our household even during the most difficult times (faith vision). All of these forms of trust exist within our relationship and have a direct effect on me. Now, to hope for my husband wouldn't have anything to do with our relationship or me. I hope that my husband gets some time to do what he enjoys or that he has a nice day.

To trust a stranger, with whom we have no relationship, means to hope that he stops at the traffic signal and doesn't run me over when I try to cross the street. Even though I trust him, I still look both ways and get a good sense that he is going to stop before I venture to cross the street. Even though we have no relationship, we have a mutual understanding and trust; my life depends on his stopping that car and this is why it's considered trust. Hope, apart from trust, would be something that has nothing to do with me. I may hope that a homeless man gets a meal and a warm place to sleep for his own benefit. I may hope that poor children are provided with food and clothing.

Hope is looking forward with a positive view through salvation in the Lord Jesus Christ. It's not dependent on circumstances or mood. When there is no hope, people feel lost and helpless. When there is hope, people feel strong and motivated. Hope comes into play most when we are being persecuted and hurt, or even when we are dying. When the Nazis took the Jews prisoner and put them in concentration camps, the only thing they had to fall back on was hope. When Jesus was being crucified on the cross, the glory and honor that He wore was hope. When a child has been diagnosed with cancer, hope is that his soul will be at rest in the Lord, whether he is miraculously healed or passes away suddenly. Hope is very important to the Christian soul; and these three remain: faith, hope, and love (1 Cor. 13:13).

PRINCIPLE   Hope is a Christian attitude unto death.

CODES	Matthew 12:21
	Romans 8:24-25
	Hebrews 6:19

44. Love Perseveres and Endures

To endure is to hold on during difficult and painful circumstances. It means doing what you must do to stay safe and sane and not giving up at the same time. It means standing steadfast to do God's will regardless of what is happening around you. If attacked by the devil, it means fighting back hard and strong and letting him know that Jesus already won the war in us. If kidnapped by a stranger, it means going on with life as God intended, despite the pain.

Suffering builds perseverance (Rom. 5:3); it makes us strong and helps us walk faithfully with God. Job is a perfect example of a man who went through great trials and persevered. Even after losing everything he owned and suffering from a terrible illness, Job still persevered, and loved God. No matter how Satan attacked him and tried to get him to curse God, he would not sin. In the end, the Lord healed him, gave him twice as much as he had before, and blessed him with a long and full life of 140 additional years and lots of beautiful offspring.

Building perseverance helps us to die to ourselves and live for Christ. How is perseverance built? Through the testing of our faith (Jas. 1:3). Jesus showed awesome perseverance when He died on the cross, as a lesson for us. So let's now "run with perseverance the race market out for us" (Heb. 12:1, NIV). If doing God's will requires us to walk thirty miles barefoot in the snow, then that is what we must do. Nothing is impossible with our Lord. Look at Moses who led the Hebrews to freedom; forty years of wandering takes a lot of perseverance.

Modern technology is a blessing for those who appreciate it but don't fully rely on it. Just because our car breaks down, doesn't mean we stop going to work. Just because our refrigerator breaks doesn't mean we stop eating. We should find a way and move forward in God's will no matter what happens to deter or slow us down. As Christians, let us not allow technology to make us lazy or weak. The devil is always trying to stop us in our tracks. We must stand up against him and fight it. We must do God's will no matter what the devil pulls to try to stop us. This is perseverance.

When I tested for my brown belt, I had to run 6 miles to show that I had perseverance. I had to defend myself against multiple attacks in the woods on the way to and during the test. I was so tired that I was ready to give up, but I wanted that brown belt so badly that I kept on going. Finally, at the end of the day, when I felt that I just couldn't take another breath without passing out, my instructor looked me in the eye and congratulated me on getting the hardest belt in the martial arts. In the same way, we as Christians must want to be with Jesus so badly that we are willing to go through anything to get there.

PRINCIPLE   Perseverance–the secret of a winner.

CODES   2 Thessalonians 3:5
             Hebrews 10:36
             James 5:11

45. Love Never Fails

According to Webster's dictionary, to fail means many different things. It means to deceive, to disappoint, to weaken, to fade or die away, to stop functioning, to fall short, and to neglect. Because love is an action and not just a feeling, it does not fail. Christ died for us because He loved us and that action changed the world forever. If we accept Christ's love for us, then we will succeed, even unto death. His love is what saved the world and gave humankind victory despite the fall in the Garden of Eden. His love is what reunites us with God and allows us to fellowship with Him despite the fact that we sinned. His love washes us clean of impurities.

God is love (1 John. 4:8). Victor Hugo once said "To love another person is to see the face of God." To be able to love is truly a gift, it's why we are here; it's all of our purpose. It withstands time and breaks all kinds of barriers and blockades. Love conquers all. As Christian martial artists, we need to always keep in mind that love conquers all; it even conquers our enemies. This is why Jesus told us to love our enemies, to do good to those who hate us, to bless those who curse us, and to pray for those who mistreat us (Luke 6:27-28). Love is a powerful weapon and Jesus knew this long before the crucifixion.

God equips and empowers us through His love. Love is the channel by which He gives us gifts, wisdom, and strength. The power of His agape love is inexpressible, unconditional, and pure. As a spark of light has a way of cutting through layers of darkness, so does a bit of love have a way of cutting through tons of hate. We did not earn God's love; we received it as a gift. Since we received it freely, we should share it freely with others. We should not love others for their works but because they are God's creation and He put them here for a reason. Just as Christ loved those who persecuted and hurt him, we should also love. If we love in this way, we can never ever go wrong.

PRINCIPLE   Love is a foolproof power used to win.

CODES   Psalm 89:24
             Psalm 89:28
             Ephesians 3:19

Chapter 8

The Fruit of the Spirit

But the fruit
of the Spirit is
love,
joy,
peace,
patience,
kindness,
goodness,
faithfulness,
gentleness
and self-control.
Against such things
there is no law.

~ Galatians 5:22-23, NIV

46. About Fruit

Fruit is nature's array of sweet and delicious desserts. Unlike many manmade desserts, fruit is good for our health and well-being. First, it's full of antioxidants, nutraceuticals, and other vitamins and minerals that help to build our bodies' defenses against sickness and disease. Second, it's cholesterol-free and packed with fiber, which helps keep the heart, circulatory system, and gastrointestinal track in good working order. Third, it contains lots of water, which is essential for our bodies since they are 80% water. Fourth, it tastes good and is a delight to eat and consume, easing the stress in our lives and helping us to enjoy more.

Research suggests that fruit reduces the risk of many cancers, coronary heart disease, and stroke. Fruit is also believed to reduce symptoms of asthma, help manage diabetes, and delay the development of cataracts. One of the reasons why fruit and vegetables are so beneficial to our health is they are filled with compounds. For example, in addition to vitamins and minerals, fruit and vegetables contain many phytochemicals (complex plant components), like glucosinolates, flavonoids, and phyto-oestrogens. Phytochemicals are what gives color to fruits and vegetables and are a type of antioxidant known to destroy free radicals in the body that often cause disease.

Similar to nature's fruit, the Fruit of the Spirit is sweet to the soul and nourishing to the body and mind. It protects us from spiritual disease, demonic radicals, and eternal death, and it gives rainbow colors to our lives as Christians. Just as it's a blessing to have fruit on earth to eat, it's also a blessing to have Fruit of the Spirit in and around us as we walk on earth. Those of us who have committed our lives to Jesus consume and produce this fruit: love, joy, peace, patience, kindness, goodness, faithfulness, gentleness, and self-control. We have access to the seeds through salvation in the Lord Jesus Christ, and we grow the seeds into fruit through discipleship and obedience. We are healthy and strong because of the fruit that grows through and winds around our beings, and we feel good because we feed others and are fed at the same time.

As Christians, the Fruit of the Spirit is our sustenance on earth, but it's also a taste or sampler of what awaits us in heaven. In other words, knowing a little love, joy, and peace on earth makes us crave and long for the overflowing love, joy, and peace in heaven. God designed us to live on His fruit from the beginning (Gen. 2:16), so it's no wonder we crave it. Fruit is the very essence of hope that we have from the Father through our Lord Jesus Christ. It's what gives us endurance to go on living in a world full of evil and hate. As Christian martial artists, it's good that we eat lots of nature's fruit to keep our bodies healthy and strong, but it's also good that we consume and produce spiritual fruit to keep our eternal lives and the eternal lives of others in good condition.

PRINCIPLE	Fruit nourishes our bodies, minds, and souls, and those of others, sustains us while we live on earth and fills us with hope for eternal life through Jesus Christ.
CODES	Matthew 7:17 John 15:8 Galatians 5:22-23

47. Love

Love is the head of all the Fruit and the only virtue of the Fruit that is described in such detail throughout the Bible. As Christians, we must understand love. First, God is love (1 John 4:16). Second, the most important commandment is to love (Mark 12:28-31). Third, those who live in love, live in God (1 John 4:16). Fourth, we love because He first loved us (1 John 4:19).

When I started martial arts training a long time ago, my instructor told me that to learn martial arts was to learn how not to fight. I never really understood that principle until I became a Christian and began to see what it really took not to fight: love. "Love is patient, love is kind. It does not envy, it does not boast, it is not proud. It is not rude, it is not self-seeking, it is not easily angered, it keeps no record of wrongs. Love does not delight in evil but rejoices with the truth. It always protects, always trusts, always hopes, always perseveres. Love never fails" (1 Cor. 13:4-8, NIV).

Love keeps us God-centered and from getting involved in arguments and fights that are trivial and unrighteous. However, it also drives us to fight important and righteous battles because it always protects (1 Cor. 13:7, NIV), casts out fear (1 John 4:18), and obeys the Lord's commands (John 14:15). As mentioned above, God is love, but He is also a great warrior (Ex. 15:3) and defender of righteousness; He calls His children to be the same. The Bible tells us that there is a time to kill and a time to heal (Eccl. 3:3), a time for war and a time for peace (Eccl. 3:8). Only God knows and dictates these times.

Contrary to popular belief, God has called His children on many occasions to fight and to kill in the name of righteousness. If He had not, then love would not have survived in this world of wickedness and hate. Just think about Hitler or other monstrous men throughout history. In Numbers 13-14, the Israelites rebelled against what God asked them to do. They were afraid to take the land of Canaan because the people who inhabited it were big and strong and the Israelites didn't think they had a chance. They refused to trust and believe in God and His strength despite all of the miracles that they performed, so God punished them by making them wander the desert for 40 years, until that entire unbelieving generation died off.

Jesus said if you love Him, you obey His commands (John 14:15). As a Christian martial artist, God may someday call you to retreat or to fight out of love. You must listen for the call and obey it. Only God knows what it will take for love to shine and righteousness to win in any given situation. "Have I not commanded you? Be strong and courageous. Do not be terrified; do not be discouraged, for the Lord your God will be with you wherever you go (Josh. 1:9, NIV).

PRINCIPLE	The reason we are here is to be made perfect in God's love.
CODES	1 John 4:18
	Matthew 22:37
	1 Corinthians 16:14

48. Joy

According to most dictionaries, joy is a state of happiness that is evoked by well-being, success, and good fortune. When and how you experience joy really depends on how you define well-being, success, and good fortune in your life. Do you define it by what is temporary or by what is eternal? Many martial arts instructors allow their joy to be defined by how many styles they know, how many black belts they have, how many degrees they've reached, how many students are enrolled, how much money they make, how many trophies they've won, or in the case of Christian black belts, how many students have accepted Christ as their personal savior.

It's okay to be happy about the things that we have and do in this world, but it's important to realize that these things are only temporary and can vanish from one day to the next. True joy is contentment that comes from the Holy Spirit through Salvation (Ps. 51:12) and the Word of God (1 John 1:4). It comes from being born into the resurrection of Christ and into an inheritance that can never fade, spoil, or perish (1 Pet. 1:3-4). Interestingly enough "enjoy" means "in joy," implying that joy doesn't come from us and that we are not its authors or creators as some people like to think. Joy already exists, through the Holy Spirit, we just make a choice to live in it or not.

Because Christ is God's joy, to live in Christ is to walk in God's joy. Our hope is on God, His promises, and our inheritance in heaven. This isn't to say that life on earth and temporary things are a waste of time; everything we experience on earth has an eternal purpose. I like to look at life as a period of growth and development, preparation for our souls in the eternal world that we have not yet seen or touched. "In this you greatly rejoice, though now for a little while you may have had to suffer grief in all kinds of trials. These have come so that your faith...may be proved genuine and may result in praise, glory and honor when Jesus Christ is revealed" (1 Pet. 1:6-7, NIV). Think about it, if life wasn't meant to be preparatory, then why is it temporary?

Spiritual joy doesn't bring happiness 24 hours a day; in times and circumstances that are full of anguish and despair, it gives us strength. The Bible tells us that the joy of the Lord is our strength (Neh. 8:10), it tells us to **count it all joy** when we fall into trials and tribulations because the testing of our faith produces patience (Jas. 1:2-4). This doesn't mean we should be jumping for joy if we've lost our home to a fire; it means we should try our best to focus on God and His eternal kingdom while we go through the grief and anguish of having lost everything we've ever owned. It helps us to put things in perspective; to see what is temporary as temporary and what is eternal as eternal.

PRINCIPLE   Happiness is temporary, but joy is eternal.

CODES   Matthew 13:44
              Psalm 51:12
              Romans 15:13

49. Peace

One of the things that we try to accomplish in martial arts training is peace, so that we can cultivate power. Peace is like a waterfall; it's soothing to see and hear a waterfall in the forest, but is dangerous to get in the way of its flow. Like a waterfall, God gives us direction in life. We fulfill it by meditating on the Word of God, focusing on Christ, and smashing through anything that gets in our way.

In order to understand how peace cultivates power, you must understand what makes power. First, power is equal to weight times speed. The more weight and the faster the speed, the greater the power. Board breaking can be an excellent demonstration of power. There isn't a whole lot that you can do about your weight, but to put as much of your body behind the technique as possible. However, there is something you can do about your speed, and that's relaxing your muscles by finding peace. If you are worried about something, then you will not be able to relax your muscles and strike the board with a speed suitable to break it.

In the spiritual sense, peace has the same effect; it relaxes your muscles and gives you more energy to fulfill God's purpose for your life. When my students are getting ready to break a board, I tell them to (1) pray to the Lord to take all their worries and give them peace and power and (2) pretend that the board is Satan and that the Father is waiting for them behind the board. Then, I tell them to focus on God behind the board and smash Satan to pieces on their way to Him. Peace allows them focus on God behind the board, relax in the process, and reach the speed necessary to break the board.

When our lives are full of stress and anxiety, our muscles become tight and overworked and our energy is zapped. All we really want to do is take it easy, but don't know how. The Bible tells us not worry because of the effect worry has on our lives; "Don't worry about anything; instead, pray about everything. Tell God what you need, and thank Him for all He has done" (Phil. 4:6, NLT). As Christians, we need to let go of our worries and seek peace that comes from Jesus Christ, so that we can smash through Satan and be with the Father. Only when we are at peace can we focus on the things of God.

PRINCIPLE	The peace of God cultivates the power of God in our lives.
CODES	John 14:27
	Acts 10:36
	Romans 8:6

50. Patience

One thing about the martial arts is it takes a lot of patience. In many schools, it takes 3-4 years of consistent study to get a black belt and even more to become a certified instructor. You must practice the same thing over and again until it becomes second nature and natural. You must practice several times a week for as long as you are learning the arts. This is why so few people continue in the martial arts to black belt, they don't have the desire or the patience to advance.

Being a Christian takes a lot of patience, too. God tells us to have patience in suffering (Jas. 5:10), and that His promises are inherited through faith and patience (Heb. 6:12). However, it's hard to have patience in a society that doesn't like suffering and is used to being instantly gratified. "I want it, and I want it now!" is a popular mentality today. You pop a frozen meal in the microwave and it's ready in 5 minutes; you take a pill and your problems are all gone. Just think about it;

we live in virtually a suffer-free society. Everything is easy.

People in our society have all kinds of problems that stem from lack of patience. Men get involved in pornography because they don't have patience for real love and intimacy. Women have affairs because they don't have patience with their husbands. Couples get divorced because they don't have patience with each other. Fathers beat their kids because they don't have patience with certain behaviors or actions. Christians separate themselves from what is holy because they don't have patience in God.

"I WANT IT" combined with "NOW" is a death toll. It will lead you places that you don't want to go. It may make things temporarily seem better, but in the end, it will only make your life worse. Clothing yourself with God's patience is clothing you with His promises, too; "The LORD's promises are pure, like silver refined in a furnace, purified seven times over" (Ps. 12:6, NLT). As Christian martial artists, we must have patience.

PRINCIPLE   Patience is one of the keys to God's promises.

CODES   2 Peter 3:15
             Proverbs 25:15
             Colossians 3:12
             Luke 21:19

51. Kindness

The old adage "to kill with kindness" is a real spiritual principle that is found in the Bible. "Therefore if thine enemy hunger, feed him; if he thirst, give him drink: for in so doing thou shalt heap coals of fire on his head" (Rom 12:20, KJV). This scripture has real value and application for martial arts training. It means that more often than not, you can diffuse and prevent fights by being kind. Remember, in martial arts, avoiding one single fight is better than winning 1000 battles.

In a way, kindness is like God's secret weapon. It's how God uses us as temples to reach people. Just think about it— probably the most influential people in your life have been very kind to you. Kindness is what gets people's attention before anything else. Think about a time when someone went out of his or her way to do something kind for you. Did it make you feel loved, appreciated, and special? Afterwards, did you have a different impression of the person? Maybe this person wasn't someone you'd normally befriend or maybe you didn't even like the person before the gesture of kindness.

From a martial arts perspective, let's say someone is really angry with you about something you don't feel is appropriate. He is yelling and calling you names. Do you soften your voice and respond in a kind matter or do you yell back and call him names until it escalates into a fight? Nonverbal communication studies tell us that if you soften your voice and respond calmly, the other person will follow your suit. This will help diffuse an argument/fight and facilitate communication. "Listen, let's go get a cup of coffee and talk about this; I'm really sorry if I've done something to offend you and I'd like to know what I did and make amends" is going to get a much better response than "Stop yelling at me you fool and if you don't get out of my face I'm going to pound you!"

To bring kindness to an everyday life perspective, let's say you are in karate class, and you jump up to do a kick and fall on your rear-end. Everyone in class laughs at you, except for one person; this person extends a hand to help you up and says, "Nice try, my friend." Such a gesture is powerful, isn't it? It would be all the more powerful if the person who took your hand happened to be someone who you never really liked much, or who you thought never really liked you much. Kindness comes from God and has a way of opening floodgates of love into our lives. God is full of kindness (Ps. 145: 17) that is free and undeserved (Rom. 11:6). As vessels of Christ, our kindness towards others should also be free and undeserved.

PRINCIPLE	Be kind freely and undeservedly, even to your enemies.
CODES	Proverbs 3:3
	2 Corinthians 8:9
	Ephesians 1:7

52. Goodness

As Christian martial artists, we have a purpose: to serve in God's army and fight against evil in the world. Our job in fulfilling this great purpose is not to do more powerful things, but to become more powerful by dying to ourselves so that Christ can live through us. Throughout history, martial artists have used the concept of flowing water (rivers, waterfalls, title waves, hurricanes, and floods) as a metaphor for power that comes from within. Christian martial artists know this power as the Spirit and identify it by the Fruit it produces.

Goodness is a manifestation or a Fruit of God's Spirit. Being good is not about the good things that you think you do with your time, abilities, and resources; it's about relying on the Holy Spirit of God to garnish you and others with His goodness, through your life. Plain and simple, you should not endeavor to be good; you should make every effort to be a vessel for God's goodness. A Godly life is full of goodness in the Spirit (Rom. 14:17). The more you allow the Holy Spirit to flow through your life, the greater the manifestation of God's goodness.

In Psalm 23:6, David wrote "Surely goodness and mercy shall follow me all the days of my life: and I will dwell in the house of the LORD forever" (KJV). God's goodness is great and is offered to those who love and fear Him (Ps. 31:19). It's offered through all the qualities, talents, people, places, and things that God so generously gives. Furthermore, as living sacrifices, it's offered to other people through our lives, and to us, through the lives of other people. This is why the Bible says to give is to receive (Luke 6:38); it's a spiritual law that when God's goodness is offered, it's also received.

"As we know Jesus better, his divine power gives us everything we need for living a godly life. He has called us to receive his own glory and goodness!" (2 Pet. 1:3, NLT). In other words, as we die to ourselves and allow Christ to live through our lives, His divine power comes upon us. It comes into our lives and through our lives; it blesses us and it blesses other people. It flows like water and its power is mysteriously and exquisitely manifested in our beings. Goodness is the generosity of God, offered through Christ, and received by man. It's an expression of God's agape love.

PRINCIPLE   Goodness is Fruit of the Spirit of God

CODES   Psalm 86:17
1 Peter 1:4-6
Romans 12:21

53. Faithfulness

Faith means trust and faithfulness means trustworthiness. We can have faith (or trust) in others and we can be faithful (or trustworthy) to others. The difference between faith and trust is that faith is based on promises and trust is based on expectations. If I tell you that I have faith in you, it means that I know without a doubt that you will stand by your promises no matter what. If I tell you that I trust you, it means that I believe you will stand by a set of expectations that we both share under reasonable circumstances.

In a like manner, a faithful person is one who will without a doubt fulfill his/her promises against all odds; a trustworthy person is one who is expected to fulfill a set of expectations under reasonable circumstances. You have faith in your spouse because you both made each other a set of promises under a covenant. You have trust in your friend because you know him as a person and believe him to have certain values. While trust is a very strong bond, faith is much stronger. Think about it, if trust were the same as faith, then we would have no reason for covenant.

Faithfulness is more than a Fruit of the Spirit; it's the foundation of our relationship with God and the key to receiving Salvation. We should not trust in God like we would trust a friend or a coworker to fulfill his/her promises under reasonable circumstances; we should have faith in God knowing that He and His promises are unchangeable, and firm no matter what. It's by faith in God, through Jesus Christ, that the Holy Spirit and God's Word and Promises come into our lives. It's by our faithfulness to God, His Word, and His Promises that we fulfill the covenant relationship that we made with His Son, Jesus Christ.

My favorite story on this subject is the story of the Good and Faithful Servants (Matt. 25:14-30). The key to fully understanding this story is realizing that the servants had a covenant relationship with their master. Thus, the servants were expected to be much more than trustworthy with the master's money; they were expected to be faithful by investing and multiplying it as if it were their own. As it turns out, two of the servants doubled their master's money and one just hid it in the ground and did nothing with it. God does not want us to take Him, His Word, and His Promises and bury it in deep in ourselves, He wants us to live by it and use it to bring more people to Him.

As a Christian martial artist, you are more than a trustworthy Christian; you are faithful servant to God. Because of your covenant relationship, God expects more of you than just learning the techniques and acquiring rank, He expects you to use what you learn in martial arts to glorify Him and help people come to know the Lord Jesus. Moreover, He expects you to be faithful to this cause against all odds. When He sees that you have been faithful with little, He will give you more.

PRINCIPLE	Faith and Faithfulness is the foundation of our relationship with God.
CODES	Psalm 25:10

Matthew 24:45
Luke 16:10

54. Gentleness

Despite popular opinion, martial arts training can and does lend itself to gentleness. In the New Testament, the Greek definition of gentleness is "controlled power." Since water is often used as a metaphor for power in martial arts, and gentleness is controlled power, water can also be used to illustrate gentleness. While controlled water runs through a dam and generates electricity for an entire city, uncontrolled water comes in hurricanes and floods and destroys everything in its path.

In my martial arts classes, students practice controlled power in many ways. First, they develop power by hitting padded targets, body bags, and boards instead of other people. Second, when working together, students are not allowed to make contact below the belt or above the shoulders. In sparring, this means that students must learn to execute their techniques quickly and effectively within 1 to 2 inches from the head in order to get a point to that region of the body. Third, they are taught that karate is their secret and pray that they may never have to use it.

Gentleness in the Christian life is applied in much the same way. It's applied when we have the ability or are in a position to really rip into someone, but instead, we make a conscious decision to be kind and allow our power to educate rather than condemn. "My teaching will fall on you like rain; my speech will settle like dew. My words will fall like rain on tender grass, like gentle showers on young plants" (Deut. 32:2, NLT). God knows how fragile we are and doesn't want us to break before we truly understand. He calls all of us to be gentle, including His Son, whom He sent not to condemn but to save (John 3:17). "Be humble and gentle. Be patient with each other, making allowance for each other's faults because of your love" (Eph. 4:2, NLT).

As Christian martial arts, it's our duty to respond in gentleness. If someone yells, it doesn't give us a right to yell back. Likewise, if someone attacks us with a punch to the face, it does not give us permission to rip off his head. We should defend ourselves with gentle words and the least amount of force possible without jeopardizing our health or safety. When dealing with sinners or Christians who have gone astray, or when we are angry with our family or friends, we must be careful of how we respond, to teach and not condemn. Jesus was such a great teacher because He was so gentle. In John 8, a woman was caught in the act of adultery but Jesus did not condemn her; instead, He reprimanded her condemners and told her to go her way and sin no more.

PRINCIPLE	Do not be quick to condemn but quick to teach through gentleness.
CODES	Proverbs 15:4
	Matthew 5:5
	Matthew 11:29
	1 Peter 3:4

55. Self-Control

In martial arts training, self-control is extremely important. We must learn to control our techniques by not making contact with our partners, our emotions by not reacting out of anger; and our time by practicing what we learn until it becomes second nature. Without self-control, energy committed to self-defense training is in vain. In other words, martial arts tactics are useless when good judgment and wisdom is lacking. "Like a city whose walls are broken down is a man who lacks self-control" (Prov. 25:28, NIV).

As a Christian martial artist, your goal is not only to exercise your body and to learn with your mind, but to develop spiritual fitness (1 Tim. 4:7) in your entire being. Part of being spiritually fit is having and demonstrating self-control. Being a self-controlled Christian means taking your thoughts captive and submitting them to Christ (2 Cor. 10:5), as well as being careful about your words (Prov. 17:27-28; 21:23). It means training your body to be honorable and holy (1 Thess. 4:4) despite popular opinion and fads.

From how you eat to the way you dress, you are to honor to God with your body. Junk food and risqué clothing is not honorable unto the Lord and will only lead you along a negative path. What you see, hear, talk, and think about should honor God with your mind. Focusing on ungodliness will lead only to unhappiness and death. "And we are instructed to turn from godless living and sinful pleasures. We should live in this evil world with self-control, right conduct, and devotion to God" (2 Tim. 2:12, NLT).

PRINCIPLE   Self-control is vital to spiritual fitness.

CODES   Proverbs 29:11
             2 Peter 1:6
             1 Corinthians 9:25

Chapter 9

The Full Armor of God

Put on the full armor of God
so that you can take your stand
against the devil's schemes.
For our struggle is not
against flesh and blood,
but against the rulers,
against the authorities,
against the powers of this dark world
and against the spiritual forces of evil
in the heavenly realms.

~ Ephesians 6:11-12, NIV

56. The Secret of Kata (Forms)
(Ephesians 6:10-18)

Be STRONG in the Lord's power and might (vs. 10). Notice that the Bible doesn't tell us to be strong; it tells us to be strong in the Lord. This is because God knows that even if we can do 80,000,000,000 pushups, we may still not be strong enough to win a fight. Our strength is nothing compared to God's, but don't worry; when you rely on Him, you will win!

Use EVERY piece of God's Armor to stand firm (vs. 11 & 13). In other words, you cannot use just the sword and the shield to stand firm; you have to use all of it. Covered with God's Armor from head to toe, you are well-equipped and ready for any and every battle that God has you fight. Covered with all of the Armor of God, you cannot lose in life or in death.

We as Christians are fighting against INVISIBLE rulers, powers, and spirits of this dark world (vs. 12). Whether it's a bully hitting you on the playground or an attack from behind the bushes, remember, it's not the person who is the root of the problem; it's the invisible forces of evil working through that person. All are savable through the blood of Jesus Christ, if they so decide.

A KATA is an imaginary fight that consists of various stances, blocks, and strikes. As we go through kata, we imagine the fight in our mind's eye; we know what we are doing; however, onlookers do not. They see how beautiful it is, but they don't know what we are practicing or what is really going on. This makes our physical techniques secretive and invisible.

As Christian martial artists, kata is also an invisible spiritual fight. You put on God's Armor and practice your secret techniques so that you will be strong and stand firm in the Lord's power. Onlookers see how beautiful you are, but don't know that you are wearing God's Shining Armor. Evil forces see you practicing, but are overcome when they try to attack.

Body Part	Piece of Armor	Martial Arts Tech	Spiritual Power	Practical Application
Head	Helmet	High Blocks	Salvation	To protect you from invasions of the mind
Heart	Breastplate	Middle Blocks	Righteousness	To protect you from the destruction of sin
Feet	Shoes	Feet Prep and Position	Peace	To help you walk with God in difficult times
Waist	Belt	Rank (Belt Color/Degree)	Truth	To demonstrate and teach truth in your life
Hand	Sword	Martial Techniques	Word of God	To attack and defeat evil head-on, anytime & anyplace
Body	Shield	Body Blocks	Faith	To deflect attacks from Satan and his legion of demons

57. Wear the Belt of Truth

While a belt doesn't protect you from harm, it does have a few important functions. It keep your pants up when you go to work or school, it holds important items like guns and batons (if you are a police or military officer), and it displays your level of training or rank in martial arts. Your martial arts rank is an outward expression of your knowledge and ability in the classroom. It's not an "I am higher than you" attitude; rather it's an "I can teach you" frame of mind. Students are each accountable for each other's successes. Traditionally, higher-ranking students teach lower ranking students in martial arts class. Teaching is a privilege and honor for students and a duty for black belt instructors.

In addition to teaching, the burden for learning is placed on higher-ranking students. If lower-ranking students do not learn what they are supposed to learn from higher-ranking students, then the higher-ranking students are held somewhat responsible. This motivates the higher-ranking students to know their craft and teach it well. When students teach other students, it also gives instructors the opportunity to work with smaller groups at various levels. Instructors may work with brown belts one day while the green belts teach, and they may work with green belts another day while the brown belts teach. In this way, even in large classrooms, everyone gets needed personalized attention, and all students advance.

When you wear a belt in class, you are telling the world that you know martial arts and can teach certain techniques to others, but when you wear the belt of truth, you are telling the world that you know God. You make a commitment to share the gospel truth according to knowledge and revelation that

God puts into your heart. You teach with Godly words, behavior, and most importantly, actions. Christians that wear this belt don't have a bad attitude that says, "I know more than you so I'm a better Christian;" rather, they have a heart that gently speaks "I have something to teach and share with you and I know you have something to teach and share with me." Whether you're a brand-new Christian, a middle-of-the-road Christian, or a mature-elder Christian, God has given you truth to share. Just as it's your duty to teach lower ranking students in martial arts class, and make sure that they learn, it's also your duty to share God's truth, as you know it.

As Christian martial artists, our school and work belts keep our clothing of righteousness in place; our police and military belts anchor the Sword of the Spirit to our waists; and our martial arts belts display truth in our lives that we can teach and share through words, behaviors, and actions.

PRINCIPLE   Wear truth in every aspect of your life.

CODES   Ephesians 6:14
             John 8:32
             John 14:6

58. Protect the Heart with Righteousness

In Biblical times, Roman soldiers wore a breastplate to protect their hearts and other vital organs. This breastplate was made with overlapping, curved iron bands that were fastened together with leather straps. Today, police officers and soldiers wear a bulletproof vest if there is a high degree of risk, but they don't wear it all of the time; the vest is hot, heavy, and difficult to walk around in day after day. Because an attack can occur at any time, and in any place, martial artists don't depend on bulletproof vests to protect their hearts and other vital organs; instead, they learn to block strikes with their arms.

While there are many organs in the body, the heart is one of the most important. It's a hard worker and its job is to pump blood to all the cooperating parts, including the brain. If the heart stops working, then the body dies. Consequently, the heart can be defined as the transporter of life, since it pumps blood, and life is in the blood (Lev. 17:14). Just as we have a physical heart that pumps life to our bodies, we have a spiritual heart that pumps life to our souls. This is why the Bible says, "Above all else, guard your heart, for it affects everything you do" (Prov. 4:23, NLT). While someday your physical heart will quit, your spiritual heart has the ability to keep going forever, if it's well taken care of.

The Bible tells us to protect our hearts with the breastplate of righteousness (Eph. 6:14). This invisible chest covering actually protects our spiritual hearts and souls. It's not made up of iron bands and leather straps; instead, it's made of righteousness, which is the result of faith and love (1 Thess. 5:8). Righteousness does not come from doing good things and following the law; it comes from faith in Jesus Christ (Phil. 3:9). When we truly accept what Christ did for us, a breastplate of righteousness covers our chests, protecting our hearts and souls from the destruction of sin. Christ died so that we could become the righteousness of God (2 Cor. 5:21).

Unlike a bulletproof vest, we can wear the breastplate of righteousness all the time by having faith in Jesus Christ and

His love. When the breastplate of righteousness covers us, sin is unable to destroy our hearts and souls and we can live peacefully in God's everlasting love. So, block those sinful strikes to your heart with righteousness from Christ, and never lose your eternal life. Jesus came so that you could not only have life, but also have it more abundantly (John 10:10).

PRINCIPLE	Righteousness comes by faith in Christ and protects our eternal life.
CODES	John 16:10
	Hebrews 10:38

59. Wear Shoes of Peace

While we practice techniques barefoot in order to toughen up our feet, our feet are much better equipped and prepared with shoes. Running shoes give us an advantage to move quickly. Sandals allow us to walk around in hot weather without hurting our feet. High heels give us extra height and can be used as a weapon in the event of an assault. Generally, shoes prepare us to get around and do different kinds of things on a regular basis, not only physically, but spiritually, too.

The Bible says, "For shoes, put on the peace that comes from the Good News, so that you will be fully prepared" (Eph. 6:15, NLT). There are two principles in this scripture. The first is that peace comes from the Gospel. This type of peace is not the opposite of war, as God actually condones war and encourages it when necessary; it's the opposite of worry and fret. God tells us not to worry (Luke 12:22-40). When we worry about things, we are not trusting God; instead, we are focusing on our own abilities and/or inabilities in a given situation. When we have peace, a great burden is lifted from our shoulders, as we trust the Lord to take care of our loved ones and us.

The second principle in this scripture is that wearing peace on our feet will fully prepare us. You might ask, "For what will it fully prepare us?" It will fully prepare us to WALK with God. It makes sense, doesn't it? Our shoes prepare us to walk. Walking with God isn't always easy and requires a good, strong, solid pair of shoes. It requires that we travel along many different paths and sometimes even blaze trails through lots of bush. In the physical, we need different shoes for different activities, but in the spiritual, we need only the Shoes of Peace to take us wherever it is that God wants us to go. The Shoes of Peace will enable us and prepare us to do God's will and move forward with the plans He has for our lives on earth.

When worries threaten to reign over your life and you no longer feel the peace that comes from knowing and trusting in the Lord, then stop and pray. Give your worries to God. God wants to take care of you and your worries while you focus on being a child of God and doing his will. Worrying doesn't solve any problems, so if you are a worrywart you are wasting a lot of time and energy; "Who of you by worrying can add a single hour to his life?" (Luke 12:25, NIV).

PRINCIPLE	Put the shoes of peace on your feet and walk with God.
CODES	Luke 12:31
	Romans 16:20

60. The Shield of Faith

The Shield of Faith is like a body block in martial arts and a large metal shield in the police force. By moving it up or down, right or left, it's capable of protecting the ENTIRE BODY and the WHOLE ARMOR OF GOD from vicious attacks of the devil. Faith is the covering of all God's spiritual powers; if it's the size of a mustard seed, then nothing is impossible through God (Matt. 17:20), so long as it's in God's will.

You are right with God through faith, not through the law (Rom. 3:28). Thus, it's important to keep your conscience clear and stay away from things that can deter or damage your faith (1 Tim. 1:19). You wouldn't want to expose a metal shield to hot, raging fire, or acid that can melt it away. Likewise, you wouldn't want to expose your faith to things that could cause you to doubt the Lord's existence, power, and love. Faith comes by hearing the Word of God (Rom. 10:17), not doubting it.

Without the Shield of Faith, God's Armor would not be sufficient to win most attacks of the Devil. The Devil would be able to knock the Helmet of Salvation right off your head and take the Sword of the Spirit from your hand. The Shoes of Peace wouldn't take you but a mile before the devil caught up, and his fire of lies would devour the Belt of Truth. Finally, the Breastplate would be useless without Righteousness through Jesus Christ; it would just weigh you down as you ran to save your life. Let's look at what Scripture says about Faith and all the Spiritual Powers of the Armor:

- Faith results in SALVATION of the soul (1 Pet. 1:9)

- Faith brings RIGHTEOUSNESS (Rom. 4:5)

- Faith gives us right living and PEACE (Rom. 5:1)

- Faith reveals TRUTH (1 Tim. 3:9)

- Faith is the result of hearing the WORD OF GOD (Rom. 10:17)

PRINCIPLE   Faith is key to using all of the Armor of God.

CODES   Hebrews 11:6
            Romans 1:17
            Luke 17:5

61. Protecting your Head

The Bible tells us to protect our heads with the Helmet of Salvation, not our arms, legs, face, or chest, but our heads! Have you ever wondered why? Well, the enemy accesses our bodies through our heads and his primary route of attack is through the thought processes. He tries to get us to question or think contrary to God's promises and then discreetly takes control of our lives.

In martial arts training, we don't wear helmets, but we do protect our heads with high blocks (which are symbolic of the Helmet of Salvation). How important is it to protect the head in martial arts? If you don't protect your head when someone is coming at it with a punch or a kick, you may end up with a black eye or a broken nose. If you don't protect your head when someone is coming at it with a hard object or a weapon, you may end up with a concussion or a brain injury. If someone grabs your head, or you land on it incorrectly, you could break your neck and die. While life can withstand the loss of an arm or leg, it cannot withstand the loss of the head. God provides us with the Helmet of Salvation to protect our lives from destruction.

When we put on the helmet of salvation, we put on faith and confidence in who we are in Jesus Christ. We expel the thoughts that the devil tries to slip into our minds and replace them with God's Word and Promises. In the same way that high blocks protect our physical lives, the Helmet of Salvation protects our spiritual lives, and saves us from self, Satan, sin, death, and hell. Paul tells us to protect our head by guarding our thoughts; "Finally, brethren, whatsoever things are true, whatsoever things are honest, whatsoever things are just, whatsoever things are pure, whatsoever things are lovely, whatsoever things are of good report; if there be any virtue, and if there be any praise, think on these things" (Phil. 4:8, KJV).

PRINCIPLE	Protect your thoughts from invasion.
CODES	Isaiah 59:17
	Ephesians 6:17
	1 Thessalonians 5:8

62. The Sword of the Spirit

The Sword of the Spirit (BKA The Word of God and The Bible) is the only weapon listed in the Armor of God (Eph. 6:17), which is why we bring our Bibles to martial arts class. "For the word of God is living and active. Sharper than any double-edged sword, it penetrates even to dividing soul and spirit, joints and marrow; it judges the thoughts and attitudes of the heart" (Heb 4:12, NIV). In martial arts, our martial techniques are symbolic of a sword, especially in karate since the word means "empty hand," and weapons are not used.

One of the unique things about the sword and martial techniques is that you can block just as much as you attack with them. Let's say you attack me with a punch; I can soft block the punch, and in the same swoop, counter-launch with a tiger claw to the eyes. While people often think of the sword and martial techniques as offensive, they are actually defensive, too. At the beginning of his ministry, Jesus attacked the devil and defended himself with God's Sword of the Spirit (Luke 4:1-13). The devil was so beat-up that he left Jesus after three matches lost.

Jesus never went to Seminary and He never got a Ph.D. in Biblical theology, so how did He know how to use the Sword (God's Word) so well? When Jesus was baptized, He was filled with the Holy Spirit of God (Luke 3:21-22). It was through the Holy Spirit that God's Word came alive in Jesus, and power came roaring through His life. He was able to overcome the devil in the wilderness (Luke 4:1-19), heal the sick (Luke 4:40), raise the dead (Luke 7:12-15), and get evil spirits to submit to him (Luke 4:33-36). In fact, His ministry began with the words: "The Spirit of the Lord is upon me..." (Luke 4:18, NLT).

We don't have to be Biblical scholars in order to have the Power of God. We need only accept Salvation through Jesus Christ and hear the Word of God decoded by the Holy Spirit. When we hear the Word, it supernaturally comes into us to live and grow, and the power of God is released. We can't hear the Word of God by simply reading our Bibles; we must have faith in Jesus Christ (Rom. 10:17). Why? Because Christ is the Word, "So the Word became human and lived here on earth among us. He was full of unfailing love and faithfulness. And we have seen his glory, the glory of the only Son of the Father" (John 1:14, NLT).

You can read the Bible until you are blue in the face, but if you don't hear it, if you don't have faith in what it says, if you don't have faith in Christ, then you are wasting your time trying to get hold of God's power. The Bible is the Written Word and Jesus Christ is the Living Word; the two together form a power sharper than a double-edged sword. In order to understand the secrets in the Written Word, you must have faith in the Living Word, and in order to have faith in the Living Word, you must hear the Written Word.

PRINCIPLE	The Word becomes alive and powerful when it's heard, accepted, and applied as truth.
CODES	Romans 10:17
	Luke 11:28
	Galatians 3:5

63. Prayer Power

Prayer is one of the most important tools we have as Christian martial artists. Without prayer, we are fighting in the dark. Satan does everything he can to keep us from open, honest, fervent prayer because he knows that he has no defense against it. While some people like to look at prayer as a cell phone connection to God, it's much more. Prayer is the energy field that brings God and His power into our lives and the lives of others. It's also the switch that turns on and activates the love and Armor of God that we wear over ourselves. It brings us into the presence of the Almighty Creator and makes our defenses and weapons work when we are under attack.

The Bible tells us to "pray in the Spirit on all occasions with all kinds of prayers and requests" (Eph. 6:18, NIV). This keeps us turned on and set in motion with the everlasting electrical charge that comes from God through Jesus Christ. It's because of Jesus Christ that we can fellowship with God through prayer. The power of prayer is not in the act itself, but in God, and in Christ who intercedes on our behalf. Thus, it cannot be misused or abused by Satan. Satan cannot pray and get results and neither can his pawns; they can only keep us from praying and getting results, if we let them. Demons try all the time to get us involved in occult activities and manipulate us into believing and upholding their ways, but we cannot fall when in constant prayer.

Despite the fact that the power of prayer comes from God, prayer is for us. It moves our heads and engages our hearts; it builds our faith and protects us from temptation to follow evil. The Bible teaches us how to pray and from what perspective to pray. While we are commanded to pray everywhere about everything, our prayer perspective may not always feel natural from our position in the world. For example, the Bible tells us to pray for our enemies and those who hurt us (Matt. 5:44, Luke 6:28). As I am writing this study, the USA is fighting a war against Iraq; do you get my drift? Praying for Iraqi soldiers doesn't exactly feel natural, and probably wouldn't be understood by fellow non-Christian Americans, but we are commanded to do so in the Bible.

Prayer cannot be used by Satan, or his pawns, for anything that violates God's ways, but prayer can affect people who are used and influenced by the evil one. This is why God commands us to pray for our enemies and for people who persecute and hurt us; prayer releases power in the lives of others that we cannot see or comprehend. It is pure power in the spiritual world on the spiritual battlefield between God and Satan. I pray everyday for our country and our soldiers who are fighting in the war, but I also pray for the Iraqi soldiers who are killing our men and women. I pray that they see the light of Jesus Christ and accept Him in their lives. We must learn how to pray in order to experience all its power and benefits.

PRINCIPLE   Prayer is indispensable.

CODES   Mark 1:35
             Luke 18:1
             Luke 22:41
             John 17:15

Chapter 10

The Great Warrior

Blessed be the LORD
my strength,
which teacheth my hands
to war,
and my fingers
to fight

~ Psalm 144:1, KJV

64. A Biblical Perspective of Escape

The Bible has a lot to say about escape. It tells us to escape the snares and traps of the devil, to escape temptation, and to escape sin, through the blood of Jesus Christ. As Christians, we should be professional escape artists!

We don't have to read very much of the Bible to realize that God wants us out of harm's way. He calls us to escape every kind of evil (1 Thess. 5:22). When we can't escape evil, He calls us to be undefeated (Rom. 12:21). No matter what things look like, our struggle is not against flesh and blood, it's against the rulers, the authorities, and the powers of this dark world; it's against evil forces in heavenly realms (Eph. 6:12). Just as God works through people to accomplish His will, the devil works through people, too.

While God desires that you be safe, He also wants you to understand that it's not really the attacker who is trying to harm you; it's the devil working through the attacker. It's the devil that robs, kills, and destroys. God loves you and love protects (1 Cor. 13:7 NIV). In His love, He wants you to use your mind and body to escape from harm. He gave you nerves, pain, fear, and reflexes, so that you could protect your body. Can you imagine what would happen to your hand if you touched a hot stove and didn't feel any pain? You would be seriously hurt, and God wouldn't want that to happen.

Likewise, He wouldn't want you to harm the attacker more than what is necessary to escape. If God had His way, every person on earth would be saved through the blood of Jesus Christ and would fellowship with Him in the Holy Spirit. God forgives everyone, even attackers who confess their sinful and evil ways and accept Jesus Christ as Lord of their lives. Remember, your body is not our own; it's God's temple and it does God's work (1 Cor. 3:16).

PRINCIPLE   God wants us safe.

CODES   1 Thessalonians 5:22
            Romans 12:21
            Ephesians 6:12

65. Discouraging the Devil with Confidence

Just as lions scope out easy prey, the devil works through criminals to scope out people who he thinks he can overcome with his strategies. According to criminology science, victims are often selected because they are perceived as being preoccupied, unaware, easy to ambush, weak, submissive, fearful, lacking in self-esteem, easy to control, and unlikely to fight back. Criminals often test their potential victims for these qualities before making a decision to attack.

Knowing this, you should always present yourself with confidence. One thing that you can do right away when a questionable person approaches you is let him know that you're prepared to fight. Keep your back straight, speak loudly with authority, and look him in the eye with courage Position yourself in a way that tells him nonverbally that he'd be better off if he left your presence immediately. Even if you feel scared, this is an example of how understanding your opponent, and responding accordingly, can save your life.

The story of David and Goliath is an excellent example of how we should demonstrate confidence. When Goliath tried to intimate David, David shouted at him; "You come to me with sword, spear, and javelin, but I come to you in the name of the LORD Almighty—the God of the armies of Israel, whom you have defied. Today the LORD will conquer you, and I will kill you and cut off your head. And then I will give the dead bodies of your men to the birds and wild animals, and the whole world will know that there is a God in Israel! And everyone will know that the LORD does not need weapons to rescue His people. It is His battle, not ours. The LORD will give you to us!" (1 Sam. 17:45-47, NLT). Now, that's a confident young man, in front of a nine-foot giant!

PRINCIPLE	Be confident
CODES	Deuteronomy 31:6
	Psalm 23:4
	Proverbs 28:1
	Proverbs 29:25

66. How to Fight

Assuming that a situation merits a fight, another question that we have to learn how to answer in martial arts training is how to fight. Again, the answers are found in the Christian Martial Arts Code: The Holy Bible. Obviously, we are to fight with the Armor of God and with prayer. Not so obvious is how much and how hard to fight and to what purpose and extent. Is a fight worth dying for? Is it worth killing for? What does God want and what is it worth to Him? People fight for silly reasons. God fights for our souls in the war between Satan and Himself. He fought hard and strong for us; He gave His only Son over to physical death in order to save us from sin and give us eternal life. He obviously values the human lives He created, every one of them.

The Bible teaches us to love our neighbors (Gal. 5:14) and do no harm to them (Rom. 13:10). Don't forget that everyone has a chance at salvation through the Lord Jesus Christ, even the most despicable. In terms of using martial arts, two questions that every warrior has to answer for himself, in any given situation, are (1) "If I intervene, will it be helpful or harmful to the people involved, according to God's will?" (2) "What is the amount of force necessary for my intervention to be most helpful and least harmful, according to God's will?" Sometimes all that is necessary to stop evil in its tracks is a simple joint lock, and sometimes it's death. When, why, and how are difficult questions to ask, and can only be answered through Bible study and prayer communication with God.

While we prepare how to fight, the real goal of the martial artist is to learn how not to fight. I know that sounds weird, but it's true. Learning how not to fight is learning how to choose our battles carefully. Although there are battles everywhere we look, many are senseless and even destructive. If we fight meaningless battles that waste time and energy, then we will be too tired to fight the important battles that could actually win the war. It takes Bible study and prayer communication to know when to give unto Caesar what is Caesar's and when to fight. Many well-meaning Christians have chosen to engage in meaningless battles over things that will pass away. For the Zen Buddhist, martial arts training (not to fight) is about controlling one's own emotions and actions through self-mastery, but for us Christians, it's about relinquishing our emotions (anger, fear, etc.) to God, who then directs our actions to work toward a higher purpose.

Martial arts training is a lot like Christianity, paradoxical, but actually quite methodological. The purpose of life, according to the Bible, is to prepare for eternity, but the goal of the Christian is to learn how to die to self. So we are training how to live, even though we are learning how to die. Anybody who doesn't study Christianity won't get that point. In the same way, anyone who doesn't study martial arts, won't understand how we can train to fight only to learn how not to fight. The Bible is full of paradoxes that hold great spiritual wisdom. Have you ever noticed the weakest are actually the strongest (1 Cor. 1:27) or how the last will become first (Matt. 19:30)? What about the King (Jesus) who is known as the world's greatest Servant? And then there's the lamb being led to its death before it defeats the roaring lion.

PRINCIPLE	To know how to fight is to know how not to fight, according to God's purpose. Seek wisdom through prayer and in God's Word for situational questions.
CODES	Matthew 22:21
	Mark 10:43-45
	1 Timothy 6:12

67. Prayer in the Midst of Attack

People attack and hurt us because they are under the influence of the devil in some way, shape, or form. If we ever find ourselves victim to an attack, the Holy Spirit will speak to our hearts and let us know what we are dealing with. He will urge us to pray through the power of the name of Jesus Christ and tell us what to pray. He may advise us to pray that the attacker see the truth or He may actually move us to cast out demons. Jesus and His disciples cast our many demons and healed many sick. If you ever have to pray over and cast a demon out of someone in order to escape from a sticky situation, you will also be releasing him/her from bondage, and helping him/her escape from the jaws of the devil.

The Bible tells us to love our enemies (Matt. 5:44). We demonstrate love to those who wish to harm us by praying for them. We know that people do evil things because they are under the influence of the devil. In the case of attackers, the devil has lied to them, manipulated them, or possessed them, and they have fallen into his grip because they didn't believe in or have a relationship with God. If under attack, we should escape and get away from our attackers, or at least protect ourselves from life-threatening positions, all the while praying. Once we are free, we should continue praying that the devil get out of the attackers and that the power of God come upon them and begin a work of salvation in their lives. Prayer is powerful and it can do wonders in situations where we are being persecuted, threatened, or harmed.

As a Christian, you have the power to overcome the devil and his demons (Luke 10:18-19). What you have to understand is that your most powerful weapons are spiritual, not physical. Even if your self-defense techniques allow you to escape and get away, the attacker is still under the influence of the devil and may hurt someone else. "The weapons we fight are not the weapons of the world. On the contrary, they have divine power to demolish strongholds" (2 Cor. 10:4). Certainly, blocking a punch or kick to the face and countering with a disabling technique is helpful, but let us not forgot to put on the full armor of God and pray. The Bible tells us to pray all the time, in the Holy Spirit, and to stay alert and be persistent in our prayers (Eph. 6:18; Matt. 26:41; Col. 4:2).

PRINCIPLE   Pray always.

CODES   Matthew 5:44
              Luke 10:19
              Ephesians 6:18

68. Recognizing Criminals

One of the things that we are learning in martial arts class is how to defend ourselves, our families, and our friends against the evil work of criminals. However, we can't defend ourselves against criminals if we don't recognize them, right? If we can recognize them, then we can escape from and overcome them. As martial artists, we seek to understand how criminals work, so that we can carefully devise strategies to beat them at their own game. As Christian martial artists, we train under the Master Jesus Christ who came to destroy the work of the devil.

Criminals are sinners who break the law and hurt other people in the process. They are sons and daughters of the devil (John 8:44) and they like to do the devil's work (John 8:44; 1 John 3:8). We recognize criminals by their acts and their character traits; they do bad things, but they are also hostile, grouchy, jealous, envious, angry, obsessive, physically abusive, selfish, bullying, and revengeful; they often think that they are right, and that everyone else is wrong, and swear and cuss, too (Gal.

5:19-21). Even if a criminal is nice and smiley on the outside, we can usually figure out his true intentions by looking at his acts and character traits.

Criminals are con artists; they disguise themselves, so be careful! They often pretend to be nice and smiley, to trap us, and then they turn really mean. Just like a fisherman gets a fish by putting a big, juicy worm on an invisible hook, a criminal can get us if we are not careful. He may try to lure us with some candy, toys, power, or money, or he may pretend to be a man of God and religious, when he really isn't. Criminals are sneaky and they'll try all kinds of bait to get a catch. They'll shoot us when we're down and they don't play fairly. The devil lives and works through them to get to us; he wants only to destroy us and has no boundaries in doing so.

PRINCIPLE	Look at the acts and character traits, not the actor.
CODES	Galatians 5:19-21
	1 John 3:12

69. Strategies of Defense

After Jesus was baptized and filled with the Holy Spirit, He was led into the wilderness where He was tempted by the devil for forty days and nights. In this story, the devil tried to attack Jesus from three angles to get Him to fall into a trap, but Jesus refused to fall. After each attack, Jesus had a few words of wisdom and outsmarted the devil on every measure. Finally, the devil realized that he wasn't getting anywhere with Jesus and went away. Yes, the devil went away! This story is a classic example of how we are to defend ourselves against the snares and traps of the devil.

First, the devil tried to grab hold of Jesus through the desire of the body. Jesus was hungry, having not eaten for forty days. In so many words, the devil said, "Hey, if you're who you say you are, then just turn this stone into some bread to satisfy your hunger." Jesus answered, "It is written, That man shall not live by bread alone, but by every word of God" (Luke 4:4, KJV).

Second, the devil tried to trap Jesus through the mind's desire for control and wealth. He took Jesus to a high place and showed Him all the kingdoms of the world. Then he said, "If you follow me, then it's all yours, Jesus." Jesus answered, "Get thee behind me, Satan: for it is written, Thou shalt worship the Lord thy God, and him only shalt thou serve" (Luke 4:8, KJV).

Third, the devil tried to trick Jesus through His own spiritual beliefs by twisting Scripture. He said, "If you're God's son, then jump off this mountain. Come on, are you chicken? It is written in your religion that God will send his angels to guard you and they'll lift you up so you don't hit the ground." Jesus answered, "It is said, Thou shalt not tempt the Lord thy God" (Luke 4:12, KJV).

Notice that in every response Jesus said, "it is written." He overcame the devil with the God's Word, because it's sharper than a double-edged sword (Heb. 4:12) and the only offensive weapon in the full Armor of God (Eph. 6:17). This means that we should fight our battles with God's Word, as much as we do with our martial arts techniques. When we are attacked by someone who is either under the influence of or possessed by the devil, the Word of God has power. The name of Jesus has power (Luke 10:17; 1 John 4:4). We overcome and enforce Satan's defeat in our lives through Jesus Christ (Rev. 12:11), the Living Word of God.

PRINCIPLE	The Word of God is a spiritual weapon; get it inside of you.
CODES	Hebrews 4:12
	1 John 4:4
	Luke 4:1-13

70. Strategies of our Opponents

As martial artists, we use lots of strategies to overcome our opponents. If an opponent punches us, we might step out the way, grab his clothing, and throw him over our hip. Or, we might fake him out with a surprise technique, like pretending to kick to his side, but then punching to his head instead. If our opponents don't know about our strategies, then we can use those strategies to win. However, if our opponents learn about our strategies, and what to expect, then we have to come up with new ones because the old ones won't work anymore.

Just as we have strategies to overcome our opponents, criminals and the devil have strategies to overcome us. If we learn about their strategies, and know what to expect, then they won't be able to beat us. While criminals all have the same motives, their styles and appearances can be worlds apart. This is why it's sometimes very difficult to identify a robber or a murderer; nobody suspects a nice-looking person to be so mean (Prov. 26:24). The devil likes to disguise himself and his works, pervert the ways of God, and twist the truth for his own purpose (Acts 13:10). He likes it when he gets an opportunity to use the Bible and unwitting or deceived Christian leaders to do his will. It makes him all the more powerful.

The devil has four strategies that he and his workers use to conquer people (John 8:44, 10:10): lying, stealing, destroying, and killing. He implements these strategies in careful disguise, pretending to be an apostle of Christ. It's not surprising, then, that his servants of evil masquerade as servants of righteousness (2 Cor. 11:13-15). As scary as it may sound, this means that the devil, or one of his workers, could be sitting next to you in church. If you don't know what he's up to, or how he operates, then you can be easily fooled, but if you understand his strategies and how he operates, then you have the upper hand (2 Cor. 2:11). "Be self-controlled and alert. Your enemy the devil prowls around like a roaring lion looking for someone to devour" (1 Pet. 5:9).

PRINCIPLE   Know what to expect from the enemy.

CODES   Proverbs 26:24
             John 10:10
             2 Corinthians 11:13-15

71. Strategies of Prevention

When you get that uneasy feeling in the pit of your stomach, beware. When something doesn't feel quite right about a person, be on guard. When in doubt, don't! More often than not, the Holy Spirit is trying to get a message to you through all the static. The Spirit knows the true nature of people and situations, so trust the Spirit. No matter what your senses are telling you, you have to learn to trust the Spirit. If danger lurks, pray and get as far away as possible. Your life is in a much better position if you can prevent a criminal from attacking you than if you have to defend yourself in an attack.

Crime can only occur when three elements are present: ability, opportunity, and intent. If you don't know someone well and there is any question about his/her ability and intent to attack you, then it would be wise to not allow opportunity into the picture. If a criminal has deemed you as easy prey, he may try to lure you with him to a secluded or semi-secluded place to carry out his attack. He may appear to be very nice and his reasoning may be legitimate. Don't be fooled; it could be lethal. Would you go into a lion's cage if a lion looked nice? No way! Your instincts tell you, no matter how nice he looks, that you could get eaten alive. Remember, evil lurks and seeks to devour you in every way, shape, and form (1 Pet. 5:8).

As Christians, we should not expose ourselves to harm, unless God has called us to do so. Our bodies are God's temples (1 Cor. 3:16) and He uses them to do His work. Our minds have many functions, one of which is to protect our bodies and keep them from evil. The Bible tells us in many places to be alert (Mark 13:33; Eph. 6:18; 1 Thess. 5:6; 1 Pet. 5:8). It tells us to be on guard (1 Cor. 16:13) and avoid every kind of evil thing (1 Thess. 5:22). This means we don't willfully put ourselves in risky situations when we are unprepared and evil may be waiting. We don't go running in the park, alone, with a Walkman blasting in our ears. We do not leave our house unlocked when nobody is home. We do not follow a stranger to a less populated area or approach someone in a car who asking us something.

Be smart! Think before you act. Wisdom is much better than strength and weapons of war (Eccl. 9:16-18).

PRINCIPLE   Be aware.

CODES   1 Peter 5:8
            1 Corinthians 3:16
            1 Corinthians 16:13

72. When to Fight

The Bible teaches us when to fight, when all other attempts to seek peace have exhausted and failed. "If it is possible, as far as it depends on you, live at peace with everyone" (Rom. 12:18, NIV). Notice that the scripture doesn't say "live at peace with everyone no matter what." Two conditions predispose it. The first is "if it is possible," implying that it might not be possible. The second is "as far as it depends on you," implying that there is only so much we can do to make peace. If these two conditions have been honestly met, and peace has still not arrived, then it's time to look at the heart. If faced with the prospect of a fight, ask yourself this...would it be for a Godly purpose on earth or would it be to satisfy a deep-seated pride, selfish ambition, or desire for revenge in your heart? Obviously if it's not for a Godly purpose, then you have no business starting it, engaging in it, or finishing it, regardless of the circumstances. To know what a Godly purpose is, read and study the Bible.

In every battle, at least one side is wrong. Interesting enough, what is right does not conflict with what is right, but what is wrong conflicts with both what is right and what is wrong. When selfishness and pride causes strife (Jas. 4:1-2), all sides are wrong. Proverbs 13:10 tells us that pride produces quarrels but wisdom takes advice. Do you need to take advice or do you need to engage in a fight for God's way to prevail? After all, the goal of a purpose-driven, Christian life is for God's way to prevail, not your own. When a battle is right, it's the Lord's. When David fought Goliath, the conditions were not favorable for him to win, but the battle was the Lord's and so He won (1 Sam. 17:47). When the Egyptians were holding the Israelites in bondage to slavery, again it didn't look probable that Moses would win, but God gave him the power to free every last Israelite in the book of Exodus; because the battle was the Lord's and the Lord appointed Moses to fight it, it was won without question. God parted the Red Sea, not Moses.

While most of the time, fighting is wrong, it can also be right. Take a look all the great warriors of the Old Testament. "Gideon, Barak, Samson, Jephthah, David, Samuel and the prophets, who through faith conquered kingdoms, administered justice, and gained what was promised; who shut the mouths of lions, quenched the fury of the flames, and escaped the edge of the sword; whose weakness was turned to strength; and who became powerful in battle and routed foreign armies" (Heb. 11:32-34, NIV). In the Bible, God raised up warriors to defend helpless people and to stop the practice of large-scale evil. He appointed people to fight His battles and He gave them all the strength, power, and weaponry that they would need. He gave spiritual weapons (2 Cor. 10:4), the Armor of God and prayer (Eph. 6:11-18), to win all His earthly and spiritual battles against sin, evil, injustice, sickness, and disease. We are to resist the devil (Jas. 4:7), as well as his representatives and work and all the torment he brings.

PRINCIPLE   Question: When to fight?
            Answer: When the battle is the Lord's.
CODES   1 Samuel 17:47
            2 Chronicles 20:15
            2 Corinthians 10:4

Chapter 11

The Child of God

> *How great is the love*
> *the Father has*
> *lavished on us,*
> *that we should be called*
> *children of God!*
> *And that is what we are!*
>
> ~ 1 John 3:1, NIV

73. Let's Appreciate

Children get excited about the littlest things. When I was a child, my grandfather used to bring me back coins from his business trips to Taiwan. They meant so much to me that I still have them today. It felt really awesome to have coins from another part of the world; I could only imagine what Taiwan was like, and to this day, I have never seen that part of the world.

As Christian martial artists, we need to appreciate and thank God for everything he's given to us. Not only should we be thankful for our loved ones and our possessions, but also for our heath, eyes, ears, nose, arms, legs, hands, and feet, not to mention all the other trillion things we have as His gifts. We are truly blessed to even have the luxury of learning martial arts. Many do not.

A thankful and appreciative heart is pleasing to the Lord. It's also good for you. If your heart isn't thankful and appreciative, then you probably walk around with a chip on your shoulder, thinking you deserve more instead of less, and resenting others who have more than you. You probably aren't a very happy person, either. Resentment and bitterness eat us away like acid on metal. So, get rid of all anger and bitterness (Eph. 4:31).

In my karate classes, I require that anyone who is not a recognized black belt in a style of martial arts must start out as a white belt in my class. Well, one of my students was a purple belt in another style, and although I told her that she could advance quickly, she was resentful and upset. She couldn't appreciate the fact that she was being offered an opportunity to learn The Christian Way and another style. So, she dropped out.

When you don't approach life with an appreciative and thankful heart, you miss what God has to offer you. If you ever find yourself feeling resentful or bitter, rather than thankful and appreciative, then ask God to change your heart. Look for a reason to be thankful and focus on that reason alone. You have much more to gain than lose if you can just let down your pride and appreciate.

PRINCIPLE   Appreciation is the key to happiness.

CODES   Colossians 3:15-17
             Luke 17:11-19

74. Get Open-Minded and Creative

One thing about our God is He's creative. Just look at all the different creatures that roam the earth from the caterpillar to the hippopotamus to the bacteria known as yogurt. Look at all the different kinds of people He made, and not one of them is exactly the same. Even the earth's surface is full of diversity, from oceans to mountains to deserts to forests. God created everything in the universe! Think about the vast extent of His creativity.

Nonetheless, it never ceases to amaze me when a close-minded Christian walks in the door; "You can't mix martial arts with Christianity, it's sacrilegious!" is what they usually exclaim. I simply smile sweetly and try to respond in kindness. God created the martial arts and they can be used for

His glory. God created the tree of the knowledge of good and evil, too. It was Adam and Eve who misused it, by eating its fruit and bringing iniquity upon humankind.

Man can misuse anything that God created and often does. As Christians, we really need to reclaim what is God's, which is everything under heaven (Job 41:11). In fact that's what Christianity is all about: reclaiming men and women from sin and death, and the griping jaws of Satan who lies and steals. Jesus Christ paid the price for us. All we really have to do is accept it. He will then come into our lives and change us from the inside out, making us worthy to stand in the presence of our Creator.

So, let us be open to God's creativity so that we can see things the way God wants us to see them and use things the way that He would have us use them, for His glory, honor, and praise. Kids usually don't have a problem seeing things in creative ways. They often invoke and inspire our creative ideas. In this way, we are to be more like children, open to God's creativity and light.

PRINCIPLE	Everything belongs to God and can be used to bring him glory.
CODES	Ezekiel 18:4
	Job 41:11
	1 Corinthians 10:31

75. Curiosity didn't kill the Cat

We use lots of expressions that simply don't make sense, like "Curiosity killed the cat." Well, how did curiosity kill the cat? It didn't. It helped the cat find the mouse. Curiosity is the fuel that keeps us moving forward on the path to God. It's those who question traditions and things they don't understand who discover the truth. God gave us inquisitive minds, so that we would not only ask questions, but also seek answers in Him.

I had a karate student not too long ago who would always ask me "Why?" Why do we bow in before class? Why do we punch and kick? Why do we get in a horse stance? Because I have asked and answered the same questions for myself, I was able to respond on my feet to most of her questions. However, there were always some that threw me for a loop and I didn't know how to answer. In those cases, I did the best I could and sought out the answers through some investigation and research.

Usually when children ask questions that we don't know how to answer, we respond by saying, "That's just the way it is." We don't offer thoughtful explanations or resources as to where to find answers. We don't even bother to find the answers ourselves. Instead, we blow them off, making their questions appear silly. Consequently, when children become adults, they respond in the same way and the questions never really get answered and addressed. It's easy for adults to accept things without reason or justification but not so easy for children. Children are taught by adults to accept without questioning.

God wants us to retain our childlike curiosity. He wants us to seek, ask, and inquire to learn the truth. It's only through curiosity that we uncover the truth and distinguish it from lies, sin, and death. I drive my boss crazy because I'm always asking him why. For example, recently he asked me to change something on a memo to make it less clear and vague. Since I'm accustomed to making things more clear and less vague, I asked him why...his response was because that's what his boss told him to do, for political reasons; that not everyone would agree with the reasoning behind the new policy formation.

PRINCIPLE	Seek, and you shall find. Be curious; it won't kill you.
CODES	Matthew 7:7
	Hebrews 11:6
	Psalm 34:10

76. Growing, Developing, Changing

From the time we are babies, we grow, develop, and change. God created us this way not to stop when we hit 18 years of age. While childhood growth is amazing both physically and mentally, adulthood is where we really begin to grow and develop spiritually. By the time we reach adulthood, we should be physically and mentally prepared to make smart decisions about our spirituality and give ourselves to the Lord.

In martial arts, many people think that once they hit black belt level, they don't need to train anymore. They think that all the hard stuff is out of the way and now they can take it easy and just teach for a while. Not so. Black belt is really just the beginning. When you reach black belt, you have learned all the basics, the foundational core of martial arts, and now you must take what you've learned and shape and mold it into so much more. You must use what you know to grow, learn, and teach.

Well, growing up in God is the same; we have only a certain amount of time to establish our foundation until we are expected to venture into adulthood and build a house for the Lord. When we are children, God provides the resources and establishes our foundation for us. However, when we are adults, He expects us to help by committing our time and resources so that He can do the rest. When the house (or temple) is finished, it can be used to bring people into God's presence and glory.

PRINCIPLE	God wants to build you into His temple, for others to come and find Him.
CODES	2 Thessalonians 1:3
	Ephesians 4:16
	1 Corinthians 3:6

77. In---Dependence

One of the most obvious characteristics of children is their dependent nature. When we are born, we depend on our parent(s) or guardian(s) to care for us because we cannot care for ourselves. We are completely helpless as babies, but as we grow up, we become more independent and know fairly well how to take care of ourselves in the world. While the term independence is often thought of as not needing the assistance of others to care for us, it actually means having the ability to manage the dependence process with more ease. Instead of saying, "Mommy, I'm hungry," you prepare yourself something to eat. Instead of saying, "Daddy, the water doesn't work," you call the plumber. This is known as independence (or in dependence, meaning inside of the dependence of others).

While God wants us to grow up, He doesn't want us to take the attitude that we can do it all, alone. Instead of relying on one or two people to care for us, we rely on many. We specialize in helping others in one area (our career) and rely on the rest of society to take care of us. I don't know how my television, radio, refrigerator, stove, and computer work. I have no clue how to build my house, make my car, or take care of my yard without machines like lawnmowers. If I were alone in the world, my life would be very difficult, and I probably wouldn't be able to survive. Thank God I'm not the only one, and thank God for all the people, talents, and things that take care of me. You see, God takes care of us whether we recognize it or not. The man who invented the refrigerator is a God-send, the man who manufactures refrigerators is a God-send, the man who sells refrigerators is a God-send, and so on.

Becoming a black belt doesn't make us independent of our instructors; there is always more to learn and always someone or something available to protect us when we cannot protect ourselves. Becoming an adult doesn't make us independent of God, either. We still depend on God's life essentials, His people, His things, and His love to live and fulfill our purpose on earth. No matter how many books we read or how much knowledge we cram into our heads, it's no bigger than a single cell in the universe. Therefore, let's recognize who God is and that everything and everyone around us, sustaining us, and keeping us alive is really God taking care of us. Have you ever been depressed and just needed a friend, and then someone walked in your door? Have you ever been sick and gone to the doctor, and he helped? Remember, God is the one who sent them.

So, learn to depend on God and stop worrying your life away. Do what God gave you the skill and ability to do, and let Him take care of the rest.

PRINCIPLE	God wants us to grow up in Him, not grow out of Him.
CODES	Psalm 71:6
	John 8:26
	2 Chronicles 13:8
	Psalm 62:1

78. Optimistic about Eternity

Children don't ever seem to have a problem looking at life optimistically. "When I grow up, I want to be President." "When I grow up, I want to be a martial arts movie star." "I want to be a super model when I grow up." Children really believe that they can be and do anything they want. It isn't until adulthood when they are confronted with countless obstacles and become discouraged. What once was optimistic is now better described as realistic.

However, God doesn't want us to settle for realism in light of optimism. "So we fix our eyes not on what is seen, but on what is unseen. For what is seen is temporary, but what is unseen is eternal" (2 Cor. 4:18, NIV). Life on earth is only temporary, so it doesn't matter if we ever make it to the Presidency, to Hollywood films, or to the front page of the top fashion magazines. In fact, for many of us, it's just as well we don't excel to such an extent because we might get too attached to fame and let it take over our lives.

God has a plan for your life on earth, but more importantly for your life in heaven. He has a special name and a unique purpose for you that only He knows. Consequently, you have reason to be optimistic. Even if your life compared to others may be a little grim, and even if you didn't end up fulfilling your childhood career fantasy, it's okay because it's only temporary. Life isn't about fulfilling our childhood dreams anyway; it's about fulfilling our purpose under God.

PRINCIPLE   Be optimistic for eternity!

CODES   2 Corinthians 4:18
            Matthew 6:33
            1 Timothy 6:12

79. Playtime, God's Cure-All

Being a martial artist isn't all seriousness. There's a lot of fun involved, too. Games, sparring, demonstrations, tournaments, and camps all make training and fellowship with other trainees enjoyable. We all like to play, just as much as we like to work out and break a sweat. Capoeira is probably one of the most playful martial art around; it's a game combined with martial arts techniques, gymnastics, and dancing. It's

God who gives us the ability to have so much fun with these kinds of things.

As Christians, God wants us to be playful. He never intended for us to lose the playful spirit that He gave us in childhood. He is a father who gives His sons and daughters lots of good gifts. Food is a great example. If God didn't want us to enjoy things, then He wouldn't have created so many foods and tastes. He wouldn't have created our taste buds either. Did you ever notice that He purposely linked out ability to enjoy food with our ability to maintain good health through nutrition? Likewise, He gave us the ability to relax and play, and linked it to health.

When we don't relax and play as God intended, we get a build up of stress in our bodily systems. Stress is one of the leading causes of illness in this country. It has been strongly linked to heart disease, cancer, lung ailments, cirrhosis, accidents, and suicide. In fact, research suggests that 43% of all adults suffer adverse health effects from stress and the majority of all visits to primary care physicians are stress-related. Busy people are not usually happy people. We need to take breaks from work. We need to relax and enjoy ourselves as God created us to do.

Stress gets people sick by damaging their immune systems, as well as by distracting and wearing out the body's defense mechanisms from attacking invaders. In autoimmune diseases like cancer, the body gets so confused and disoriented that it begins to attack itself, thinking that it's the actual invader. God didn't design us to be workhorses, but to have fun and enjoy life through him. Work is a necessary part of life, but so is play. Without work we may starve to death, but without play, we may destroy ourselves.

PRINCIPLE	Both work and play are essential for God's children.
CODES	Psalm 16:11
	Psalm 90:15
	Psalm 96:11-12
	Psalm 150

80. Rules have a Purpose

Rules, rules, rules; everywhere we look are rules. There are rules at home, rules at school, rules at church, rules on the street, rules at work, rules at play, rules in automobiles, rules in planes, rules for games, rules for bike riding, rules for walking, and the list goes on. Obviously, by the sheer volume we live with, rules are an important part of life for kids and adults. Like martial arts, their purpose is to protect. About a year ago, the state where I live enacted a new law that every person in a car be required to wear a seatbelt, in addition to all the other laws that govern automobile operation. If a police officer catches anyone without a seatbelt, then the driver gets a ticket. Believe it or not, lots of people are getting tickets because they don't do what is necessary to protect themselves or their loved ones in a car. Likewise, people get kicked out of martial arts class because they don't want to follow the rules that govern behavior, by misusing techniques outside of class, making contact when prohibited, etc.

In addition to all the written and spoken rules that govern our behavior, there are unspoken rules, too. Standing in line to wait for something is an unspoken rule in our country/culture. People who cut in line or push and shove their way to the front are considered violators of this rule and get a bad reputation, which is not necessarily the case in other countries and cultures. I lived in Cameroon a long time ago, where people don't believe in standing in lines. At my bank, I had to push and shove my way to the front in order to withdraw money because that's what everyone else did. Even when I made my way to the front, it wasn't always guaranteed that I'd get what I wanted or needed. If I asked to withdraw $20, the teller would ask me "What for?" If my reason was valid, in her mind, then she had the authority to give me some of my own money. If it wasn't valid (in her mind), then she also had the authority to give me less than I requested or deny my request altogether. Needless to say, it was very difficult to live in Cameroon.

It's always hard to live in other countries. We experience culture shock because the rules are different than our own and it takes awhile to get used to them. We get used to them and adjust or we don't get used to them and leave. Because people do not know our rules, they disregard them, and we feel violated and hurt. At the same time, we are expected to follow their rules no matter what. When a US citizen goes into another country, he/she is subject to the laws of that country. Breaking laws in a foreign land can result in very serious consequences. There is little the US government can do to help you if you get into trouble with another country's legal system; you will be subject to their judicial courts and their punishments, which are usually stiffer than what you are used to in the United States. Even if innocent, you may get life in prison for a drug charge because someone else set you up indiscreetly. Even if you didn't know you were breaking a law, you are responsible, so know the laws and rules of everywhere you go.

As Christians, we are obliged to follow one set of rules, God's Law under Christ (Gal. 6:2). His Law is made up of more than the 10 Commandments, it's the entire Bible, which can be summarized in two simple directives; "Master, which is the great commandment in the law? Jesus said unto him, Thou shalt love the Lord thy God with all thy heart, and with all thy soul, and with all thy mind. This is the first and great commandment. And the second is like unto it, Thou shalt love thy neighbour as thyself. On these two commandments hang all the law and the prophets" (Matt. 22:36-40, KJV). As Christian martial artists, we agree to follow the Law under Christ and keep it in our temples (our bodies, minds, souls). We agree to teach others about the law, too, as well as the benefits like true freedom (Jas. 2:12). God's Law sets us free from the Law of Sin and Death, the law that rules the earth. Consequently, as Christians, we should know what it's like to live in a foreign land; after all, we live on earth.

PRINCIPLE	Rules are supposed to set free, not constrain. The Law of Sin and Death constrains, the Law of God sets us free.
CODES	Romans 8:1-4 James 1:22-25 James 2:10-13

81. What's Teachable is Reachable

Like little children, God wants us to be teachable. He doesn't want us so set in our ways that we cannot move or change. Teachable moments are found in things that adults often overlook. What fascinates a child is dull routine for adults. Nonetheless, from the day we are born to the day we die, life is about learning. Like clay in a potter's hands, we are shaped and formed through learning into beautiful pieces of work to serve the Lord; we are formed into vessels of mercy, honor, and glory for His Spirit to dwell (Rom. 9:13-24).

As martial arts students, we must also be teachable like children. We must be willing to spend the time and energy necessary to learn what it takes to advance in rank and knowledge. How many times did you have to go over the same techniques in order to get your first belt? Likewise, how many times do you think you will have to go over the same technique to get two more belts? We may have learned how to perform it the first time with form, but now it's with speed and power. Later, it's bringing form, speed, and power into unity with each other to make the technique crisp and clean.

You may have discovered ages ago what it means to be a Christian, but most likely, you're still learning how to die to yourself and allow Christ to live through you. I accepted Christ as my personal Savior about 15 years ago, but it has really just been in the past few years when I've begun to trust Him enough to give Him my heart. How? By letting Him into every part of my life. I don't know it all, and I never will, but God continues to teach me because I've allowed Him to reach me. As children reach out to learn from us, so should we reach out and learn from God.

PRINCIPLE	We are only teachable to the extent that we are reachable.
CODES	Proverbs 19:20
	Matthew 11:29
	Job 34:4

82. Watch the Joyous Children

Children are always bursting with joy. When the little tikes come into my classroom before the official start of class, they are so excited. They are running around and tagging each other, telling me stories about their week, and just so happy to be alive. The joyous spirit in children is truly admirable. I always pray that I can be as enthusiastic as they are about karate class and life.

God doesn't want us to lose the joy He gave us in childhood. He wants us to be happy to be alive and living for Him in His glory. Granted, true joy is not always the same as happiness; it's peace of mind and heart regardless of circumstances. It seeks nothing more than to please the Lord and is content simply by living in the presence of God. Joy comes from God and the Word of God. It can only exist when we surrender ourselves to God, under all circumstances (Jas. 1:2-4).

Even children who do not live under what we would call positive life circumstances also manage to discover joy through God. They trust Him easily because they cannot and do not have the power yet to take care of or trust themselves. As adults it's harder for us to trust the Lord because we are taught to take care of our own problems, and ourselves, or rely on others to do it for us. When we let down the walls and trust Him, God rewards us for our obedience by giving us joy.

PRINCIPLE   Let God make you joyous like children.

CODES   John 15:11
                1 John 1:4
                Habakkuk 3:18

Chapter 12

The Great Commission

And he said unto them,
"Go ye into all the world,
and preach the gospel
to every creature"

~ Mark 16:15, KJV

83. At Your Service

The goal of our fulfilling the Great Commission is to save souls, by bringing them to the Lord Jesus. However, before we can save souls, we have to soften hearts. Nobody ever saved a soul by scaring people to death and filling them with so much fear that they don't know what to say or do.

Hearts are softened by service. That's why so many missions groups go into the world to help people build houses, improve communities, vaccinate children, etc. It's through service that the Fruit of the Spirit blossoms and the gates of the kingdom of god are opened into the lives of His children.

Think about a time when someone helped you and how it changed your life. Think about a time when you helped someone else and how it changed his/her life. Have you ever defended someone who couldn't defend himself? Have you ever stood up for someone who was getting picked on? Have you ever helped your neighbor? If so, how?

"Be dressed ready for service and keep your lamps burning, like men waiting for their master to return from a wedding banquet, so that when he comes and knocks they can immediately open the door for him" (Luke 12:35-36, NIV). Christ said that no one who takes hold of a plow and then looks back is fit for service in the Kingdom (Luke 9:62).

PRINCIPLE   The kingdom of God is a kingdom of service.

CODES   Ephesians 4:11-13
             2 Corinthians 9:12
             1 Timothy 6:18

84. Can we get a Witness?

In a court of law, a witness is someone who can provide evidence in favor of or against a plaintiff. He or she has firsthand information about something that the rest of us do not have. Witnesses are very important for prosecuting criminals and releasing those who are accused but innocent. Without witnesses, the legal system would be crippled and/or corrupt, unable to keep our communities safe because criminals would walk free. If this were the reality, we would be completely dependent on ourselves for our safety, as the people of East Asia were centuries ago when they secretly developed martial arts.

Being a Christian is similar to being a witness. We have firsthand information about something that the rest of the world doesn't necessarily have. Consequently, it's our duty to share that information carefully and judiciously to protect other people. We know Jesus Christ personally and we know what He did for the world. We know that Jesus Christ is the only truth, way, and life (John 14:6) and that nobody can get to the Father except through Him. There are plenty of false witnesses who say that they are the way or there is another way, but they are deceived and deceiving. It's our job to set the record straight with true testimony.

As Christian martial artists, we have powerful testimony. Christ is our Master and we follow Him. Christ is our Savior and we bow down to Him. Christ is our Redeemer, and we grow and change through Him. While we have witnessed many of the same things as Christians, we have witnessed different things through Christ, too. Because we have a personal relationship with Jesus Christ and the Father, He reveals his personal thoughts to us that other Christians may not even know about or understand. It's our job to seek what God wants us to do with His revelations in our lives.

A personal thought that God shared with you could be found in a unique way that you interpreted a scripture in the Bible. It could be in the way you understood a message that a preacher shared. God may have intended this thought to be just for you or He may have given it to you to share. Maybe this thought is something that mainstream Christian society has been longing to hear or maybe it's something that isn't accepted by mainstream Christian society, but represents truth that God wants revealed. These are questions that Christians have to ask themselves.

Throughout history, God has given mankind thoughts that they wrote down and developed. The Bible is written by both men and women, and is told to be the inspired Word of God. "All Scripture is God-breathed and is useful for teaching, rebuking, correcting and training in righteousness, so that the man of God may be thoroughly equipped for every good work" (2 Tim. 3:16-17, NIV). *The Purpose Driven Life* by Rick Warren has sold over a million copies and has changed countless people's lives because God gave Mr. Warren a thought and asked him to develop and share it. Who would have thought that one could mix Christianity and martial arts?

PRINCIPLE	God shares personal thoughts with us through the personal relationship that we have.
CODES	Proverbs 12:17
	Acts 10:43
	2 Timothy 1:8
	2 Corinthians 5:17-21

85. Communication and Culture

Culture is the way that we understand and behave in the world. It's very complex and consists of our language, political views, economic status, psychological profile, religious beliefs, nationality, race, sex, and more. Sights, sounds, smells, tastes, and even touch are filtered through the frames of our culture before they are translated into meaningful pieces of information in our lives. This filtration process is called worldview.

In order for us to do God's will in a world of differences, we have to be able to communicate through different people's worldviews. Beyond understanding what people think, we have to understand how they feel, and how they might react to information. In some African languages and thought, there is no future tense. How do you talk about heaven to a people that don't think in terms of the future? Carefully slipping through other people's worldviews is the only way.

Christ instructed us to be agents of cultural change (Matt. 28:20). By mere virtue of your participation in Christian martial arts, you have accepted this teaching as truth. With God's blessings, Christian martial artists have carefully tapped into an Eastern cultural forum just enough to transform it in motivation, but not in content. This is the job of a missionary, not to destroy or do away with a culture, but to make it Christian and orient it towards God.

It's not the answer to do away with martial arts, or any cultural forum that doesn't explicitly violate God's ways, but rather work to make it Christian. Jesus worked within the framework of many people's cultures to help them come to know the Father. Scripture exists in about 2500 different languages and there are numerous translations in each language. Christ told us to go to the ends of the earth and preach the Gospel, not to bring the ends of the earth to us. Certainly, He meant more than physical relocation.

PRINCIPLE	Be a transformer of culture, not a destroyer of culture.
CODES	Matthew 28:20
	1 Corinthians 9:19-23

86. Flexibility To Stretch

Stretching out before class loosens up our body and prepares us for a tough workout. If we don't stretch our bodies before we start doing all sorts of techniques in class, then our muscles and ligaments are susceptible to tears and breaks. Muscles and ligaments are like rubber bands, the older they become, the stiffer they get, unless they get used with frequency. The other day I took a rubber band out of my drawer and tried to wrap it around some envelopes; before it reached half way around, it snapped and broke. The rubber band didn't break because it was too small; it broke because it had been sitting for a long time without use and was suddenly stretched with force.

For the same reason that we strive for flexibility in class, the Bible teaches us to be flexible in life. In class, we don't want to pull our muscles or ligaments and in life we don't want to rub others the wrong way. Our goal is to attract other people to Christ who lives through us, not turn them away. If we are turning others away from us, then we are not living as Christ intended. If you've ever traveled to another country or culture, then you know what flexibility in life is all about. The old proverb says "When in Rome do as the Romans do." We have to put ourselves in other people's shoes and communicate with them at their level if we expect to befriend them and reach them with the Gospel. People don't listen to people on holy high horses; they listen to their friends.

Missionaries are experts at being flexible and communicating across cultures. Forced to go into countries where cultures are very different from theirs, they must do all they can do to reach people. They must learn languages and customs; eat food that they are not accustomed to eating; live without modern-day conveniences and comforts; and work harder just for the bare necessities (like water). When I was in the Peace Corps, I knew a foreigner who refused to do any of this; he was much like a joker who was pretending to be a king of hearts. He drove a very nice SUV among people who didn't even have cars and fed his dogs better food than his neighbors ate. The Africans made jokes about him and wondered why he was even in their village. Let's not be like this man; let's be flexible.

PRINCIPLE	Flexibility in life will give you a much better stretch.
CODES	1 Corinthians 9:19-23

87. The Kingdom of God

Storytelling is one of the most effective ways of teaching that mankind has ever known. Jesus used all sorts of parables to teach us how to live as God's children. Many martial arts instructors use them to teach principles to students, also. When I was in college I thought I had a good understanding of Christianity and the Bible. I thought I knew the difference between heaven and hell, and then I heard a story from China that helped me understand the difference better.

Once upon a time there was a man. Because of his heart, the Lord answered one of his deepest prayers. He prayed for a chance to see heaven and hell before he died, so that he could write a book about the difference. So, the Lord sent an angel to take the man to visit hell. What a strange place; it was not hot and full of fire as he imagined! It looked like a big room, with tables of delicious food. There were steaming hot plates of chicken, beef, shrimp, fish, vegetables, rice, noodles, casseroles, and desserts. However, nobody was eating any of this good food. The people sitting around the tables looked as if they were starving. They were holding chopsticks that were so long that they reached across the table, making it impossible to bring the food from their plates to their mouths.

Then, suddenly, the Lord sent an angel to take the man to visit heaven. Amazingly, heaven looked just like hell, with lots of tables covered with wonderful food, and people holding super-long chopsticks. It wasn't full of gold and silver or anything else of glamour. There were just people having a good time around the food. While in hell, everyone was starving in the midst of this good food; in heaven, everyone was eating happily, and laughing together. The man looked and wondered why. Then he saw and understood the true difference between heaven and hell. In hell, the people were trying to use their long chopsticks to feed themselves, but couldn't get the food in their mouths. In heaven they were using their long chopsticks to feed each other.

Before I even started training in martial arts, the political arena was a lot like hell, and it still is. Just look around... you'll find countless different styles, associations, and leaders supposedly representing the same things, but trying to feed themselves and their egos in lieu of others. Big commercial schools, lots of money coming in, expensive uniforms and equipment, and unfair ranking all make the politics of martial arts a mess. You'll find this mess in the Church, too. People in high places, fighting like cats and dogs and doing whatever they can do to get a leg up, above others, and make their ways stand out as supreme. Someday, when the world is a different place, when the Kingdom of God reins on earth as it does on heaven, men and women will work together to accomplish bigger purposes, beyond themselves, rather than trying to feed themselves, alone.

Jesus Christ is a perfect example of heaven because He works with us to accomplish His purposes, not against us. He comes into our lives to make His body bigger and stronger, and stretch further through humanity, while we become bigger, stronger, and stretch. He works through us, not around us or above us, and shines forth His love to all those who are willing to receive it. He came to give us life, not put His life first. To God, we came first when He walked the earth, and we still come first as His Son dwells within our beings. Christ fed us and He still feeds us. In doing so, He is fed, His body is made bigger and stronger, and His purpose reins forever more. Christ understands how the Kingdom of God works and His goal was and is to bring the Kingdom to earth forever.

PRINCIPLE   In God's Kingdom, we feed others and others feed us, and this is how we are sustained.

CODES   Matthew 6:9-13; 12:26; 13:44
          Luke 13:20-21
          John 3:3

88. Light of the World

So who are we and what are we here for? Why doesn't God just zap all Christians up to heaven right now to be with Him? What's the point of living here on earth? These are tough questions, but the Bible contains answers. We are the light of the world. We are here for others, that through the light we give off they might see a glimpse of, come to know personally, and glorify God. We are here as vessels for our Lord God to attract others to His light and subsequently save souls.

As the eye was created to function in the light, man was created to function in God. The eye doesn't function correctly in darkness and man doesn't function correctly in sin. God is found in the light and sin in the darkness. Because there was so much darkness and no light left in the world, God had to enter the world Himself to bring back the light. God sent Jesus Christ into the world so that we could, through Him, find our way back to the light and God. He loved us so much that He wanted to give us a chance to come home.

Jesus came into the world as a torch. He brought light into the world and lit up many other torches through His teachings and sacrifice. He continues to light up the world through those who accept Him as Savior and commit their lives to His work and purpose. His light shines through all believers and He ignites new people with His light daily. The result is a domino effect of lights popping up all over the world and cutting through the darkness. One day, the darkness will be gone forever. One day, there will be nothing around us but light from the kingdom of God and we will be able to rest in Him.

If you have invited Jesus into your life, then you are a light in the world, a torch burning through the love of Jesus Christ. Christian martial artists are torches and provide light to many. Jesus uses our skills and talents to bring His light to people who otherwise may never see it. While a light can cut through darkness, it is limited in scope and can only travel so far. Someone has to be a light in the church, someone else at school, another in the prisons, and so on. We are the body of Christ, designated by God to do His work on earth. It's through the covenant we have with Christ that God uses us to save sinners.

PRINCIPLE	Christians are lights in the world.
CODES	Matthew 5:14-16 Acts 13:47 Romans 13:12-14

89. The Christian Commission

A commission is an assignment of authority to act for, in behalf of, or in place of another. With this in mind, think about the Great Commission and what Jesus assigned us to do on earth. The Great Commission is commonly taught as preaching the Gospel to all nations, as commanded in Mark 16:15 and Matthew 28:19; however, it's more. The purpose of Christian life is to work for the Kingdom of God. God didn't necessarily put us here to spend eight hours a day flipping hamburgers or counting cash for a capitalist corporation, but to work His vineyard (Matt. 21:28).

God's vineyard is composed of this world. As Christians, we are commissioned by God to act as living sacrifices for Jesus Christ to continue His work in this world. Jesus is God's son, but He is also God's servant. When we accept Jesus as our Savior, God adopts us as a son or daughter, but He also adopts us as a servant. Every Christian that has ever invited Jesus Christ into his/her life has been assigned to take an important, active role in the work of winning the world for God. God made men and women into apostles, prophets, evangelists, pastors, and teachers to build up the body of Christ (Eph. 4:11-12).

So what kind of work are you supposed to be doing? Well, you know, it really doesn't matter. You could teach martial arts, work in a grocery store, or help little kids cross the street. Whatever you end up doing, just listen to Jesus Christ: "You are the light of the world—like a city on a mountain, glowing in the night for all to see. Don't hide your light under a basket! Instead, put it on a stand and let it shine for all. In the same way, let your good deeds [work] shine out for all to see, so that everyone will praise your heavenly Father" (Matt. 5:14-15, NLT). God's work can be manifested anywhere, anytime, and through anything we end up doing, as long as Christ lives in us.

While we are not saved because of our works, we are created and chosen for works (Eph. 2:8-10). This means that we can't earn our salvation through the works we accomplish, but as Christians we can and should be instruments for God's work to flourish in this world. We are His workmanship and we do His work. Jesus Christ came to do more than save us from our sins and death; He came to show us how God wanted us to work. Jesus was not a representative of God's glory; He was God's glory. Metaphorically speaking, Jesus was like a beautiful clay pot that poured God's work into the world. There was nothing in Jesus that stopped the flow of God.

We are all meant to be God's beautiful clay pots, to pour Him into the world. As Christian martial artists, we know that Jesus Christ is our only hope to become what God intended for us to be. Our ideals are the Word of God and our objective is to become instruments for Jesus Christ to continue his work in the world. When we give our hearts to Jesus Christ, He cleans up the convoluted mess inside and frees the spout in our lives that allows God to pour into the world. And so it's written, "greater is he that is in you, than he that is in the world" (1 John 4:4, KJV). Greater is Jesus Christ who lives in you, than Satan, the ruler of the world system. Together, you and Jesus can accomplish the Great Commission for God.

PRINCIPLE   The Great Commission is in you. Let it work
              through your life.
CODES   John 5:17-34, 9:4, 14:10, 17:4

90. Presentation Counts

When I was a teenager, I heard a story from Japan that forever changed the way I looked at martial arts and myself as a fighter and a Christian. The story is about presentation, how to present ourselves to people who prejudge us, treat us with disrespect, or bully us without reason or rhyme. I had heard that first impressions were the most important, but never really thought about it terms of martial arts until I heard this story.

Once upon a time there was an artist of the tea ceremony who often presented in the palace of the Lord Tosa. One day the Lord Tosa took the artist, along with his samurai, to visit the Shogun in the city. The Shogun had a custom that every man who entered his palace must be dressed in the traditional attire of the samurai warrior. So the artist had to dress up in costume and carry two crossed swords.

When the artist was taking a break and walking around outside, a mean-looking mercenary bumped into him and the artist fell down. When the artist got up and started walking away, the mercenary yelled at him, "How dare you push and shove me around!" The artist was a bit taken, since it was the mercenary that pushed him, not the other way around. "Excuse me," said the artist, "but it was you who knocked me to the ground."

The mean-looking mercenary became irate and challenged the artist to a fight. The artist tried to decline, saying that he wasn't really a samurai warrior; he was just dressed in costume for a presentation in the Lord's palace. But the mercenary wouldn't take "no" for an answer and told the artist that if he didn't accept, then the mercenary would spread rumors that the Lord Tosa is served by men with no honor.

The artist had no desire to fight but because he didn't want to dishonor Lord Tosa, so he accepted on one condition. The artist asked for two hours to take care of some personal business. The mercenary agreed and assured the artist that if he didn't come back in two hours, the rumors would begin. So, the artist ran as fast as he could to the nearest sword-fighting academy to learn how to hold a sword properly so as to die with honor.

When the artist explained his dilemma to the head swordsman, the swordsman chuckled. "Why are you laughing?" said the artist. The swordsman explained that most students come to learn how to kill their enemies, and avoid death, not to learn the art of dying. However, he agreed to teach the artist anyway. "Before I reveal my art to you," said the swordsman, "would you show me your art?"

The artist knew this would be his last opportunity to lead a tea ceremony. So, he did his very best. He assembled the utensils: the brazier, the clay vessel, the whisk, the water, and the tea, and then he prepared himself to peacefully serve tea to the swordsman. As the swordsman observed the artist, he said, "You are already prepared. I have nothing else to teach you." The swordsman then continued to explain to the artist what he meant.

"When you to fight, approach this mercenary as if he is your good friend. Treat him as one of the most honorable guests at your tea ceremony. Greet him politely, thank him for waiting, take off your jacket, and place it next to him. Tie on your headband, face your opponent, place your sword over your head, and close your eyes," said the swordsman. The swordsman then assured the artist that all would be as he desired and he would die an honorable death.

When the artist went to fight the mercenary, there were all sorts of people around pumped up with adrenaline, anxious to see a good fight. He did everything that the swordsman told him to do. The artist greeted him politely, thanked him for waiting, took off his jacket, and placed it next to the mercenary. He then tied on his headband, faced his opponent, placed his sword over his head, and closed his eyes. He had no tea to serve, only himself.

The artist waited for a while but nothing happened. Finally, he opened his eyes and was astonished to see the mercenary's sword on the ground in front of him. The mercenary backed away slowly, with eyes full of terror, and then turned away and ran. When the mercenary had seen the artist standing peacefully in front of him, he couldn't go through with the fight. He didn't know how to attack a peaceful man, waiting to serve his whole life as he normally serves tea.

PRINCIPLE	The way we present ourselves has a lot to do with the way people respond to us.
CODES	Titus 2:6-8
	2 Timothy 2: 23-26
	Romans 12:9-21

91. Talents and Gifts

This lesson is the only one that requires you to read the codes first (before class). If you haven't read them yet, then take about five minutes to read them before proceeding. The *Parable of the Talents*, *Spiritual Gifts*, and *One Body with Many Parts* all demonstrate the responsibility that we have as Christians to use the talents and gifts that the Father gives us to further His kingdom on earth. Our purpose on earth is to use what we have and make the best of it to do the will of the Father.

God has given you talents that He has given no other. Maybe you have the best sidekick on the planet. Maybe you can break a board with your pinky. Or, maybe you are just average at martial arts, but have a talent for bringing concepts to life through careful study, research, and writing. Whatever your talents, God wants you to use them to further His kingdom on earth and in heaven. He wants you to use what He commissions you to do. Don't bury your talent; even the smallest measure of talent can be used in big ways, to glorify God and bring people to His light.

God has given you spiritual gifts and wants you to use them in the body of Christ. One person's spiritual gifts may seem trivial compared to another's, but remember that both are essential to fulfilling God's will on earth. The parts of the body that appear to be weaker are actually indispensable (1 Cor. 12:22) and necessary for the bigger parts to function. You are important to God, but also for God. God depends on you to do what He made you—and only you—capable of doing. Don't hide yourself; come out of the dark, and eagerly seek greater gifts (1 Cor. 12:31).

PRINCIPLE	Talents and gifts are to be used for God's glory, not ours.
CODES	Matthew 25:14-30
	1 Corinthians 12

Chapter 13

The Christian Black Belt

Righteousness will be
his belt and faithfulness
the sash around his waist.

~ Isaiah 11:5, NIV

92. Child of God

Jesus said that unless we change and become like little children, we will never enter the kingdom of heaven (Matt. 18:3). What did He mean by this? After all, Paul said that when he became a man, he put childish ways behind him (1 Cor. 13:11). Dependable, teachable, and inquisitive are some qualities that we are supposed to hang on to even as we grow into adults, leaders. As strong and courageous as a giant warrior, yet as dependable and teachable as a small child, is the true spirit of a Christian black belt. We must always be teachers while never ceasing to be students. We shouldn't ever think we know it all.

No matter how many martial arts styles, techniques, or forms that you know; no matter how many black belts you receive, you will never know it all. No matter how good you think your sidekick is, there is always room to make it better. We are not perfect and can never be perfect, we can only commit our lives to one who was and is perfect (Jesus Christ). We can never even understand or comprehend perfection, but we can aim for it from where we stand. "Let us fix our eyes on Jesus, the author and perfecter of our faith, who for the joy set before him endured the cross, scorning its shame, and sat down at the right hand of the throne of God" (Heb. 12:2, NIV).

As a father leads and directs His children, and expects responsibility out of them as they grow older and more mature, he still wants them to depend on him as father. And so does God...He expects more responsibility out of us as we mature but never expects us to cease learning and growing in Him. I am now a black belt instructor and a parent, yet I still go to other instructors to learn more about martial arts and my parents to learn more about parenting. Isaiah 37:30 tells us about the three seasons of life and the Christian walk. First we eat what grows by itself; then, we eat what springs from that; and finally, we sow and reap, plant vineyards and eat their fruit. Although we acquire responsibility over time, we still depend on God to make vineyards grow and produce fruit from seed.

PRINCIPLE   God calls us to be childlike, not childish.

CODES   Ephesians 5:1
             1 John 3:1
             Mark 10:15

93. Discipleship

What is a disciple? A disciple is one who believes, follows, and supports a school or individual. More than a student; he/she recruits others to believe and follow as well. We can be disciples of anything or anyone. Martial artists are disciples of different styles and schools of martial arts. Christians are disciples of different denominations and churches. Volunteers are disciples of different causes. Disciples are disciplined and dedicated and they are usually very enthusiastic about their discipleship. They make great sacrifices of time and energy to proclaim their beliefs and seek support from others.

Being a disciple of Christ requires sacrifices. In fact, Jesus clearly outlined these sacrifices in the Bible. "If anyone comes to me and does not hate his father and mother, his wife and children, his brothers and sisters—yes, even his own life—he cannot be my disciple" (Luke 14:26, NIV). We have to be willing to give up everything and everyone for God, including our own lives. In Genesis 22, Abraham was unsuspectingly tested on his discipleship; God asked him to sacrifice his only son, and he did not withhold him from the Lord. Just before the sacrifice, the Lord stopped Abraham and told him that he passed the test. Then, He promised to bless Abraham and his descendents abundantly.

In addition to "willingness" to give up everything and everyone, we must also carry our cross and follow the Lord Jesus Christ. "And anyone who does not carry his cross and follow me cannot be my disciple" (Luke 14:27, NIV). Interestingly enough, Jesus taught this requirement of discipleship before He was crucified on the cross. So, what exactly did Jesus mean? As we know from the Bible, the Romans used the cross to put criminals to death in the first century. As we also know, spiritual death is the result of sin. Jesus was telling us to crucify our flesh (sinful nature which kills and destroys us) and follow Him. Carrying our cross, or the crucifixion of our flesh, implied that it was an ongoing process, a journey to freedom. It could not be obtained by standing still and lingering.

Jesus was telling us to pick up our cross and carry it while we followed Him, not to let it weigh us down and kill us. Jesus knew that if we could take hold of our flesh and follow Him and His way, then there would come a time and place along the path when He would begin to help us carry it and soon take it away completely. Jesus physically carried His own wooden cross to the crucifixion (John 19:17), but He spiritually carried ours. He carried the sinful nature that would have killed our souls, so that we could be free at last. Because He was God and man at the same time but without a sinful nature, His death served as the ultimate sacrifice that took our cross and sin. He saved us from death because He took our place on the cross that we would have died on and set us free.

PRINCIPLE	Christian black belts should be disciples of the Lord Jesus Christ.
CODES	Matthew 10:38-39
	Luke 9:23
	Galatians 6:14

94. Leadership

To be a leader is to go against the norm and take others with you. Leaders start out as followers. Jesus spent the first thirty years of His life following before He ventured out to lead. Likewise, the twelve disciples spent three years following Jesus before they went their separate ways to lead. Martial arts instructors have to spend time following a curriculum to black belt before they can lead a martial arts program or school. Christian martial arts instructors must spend time in the Word of God before they can teach the Christian way through martial arts.

While leaders must start out as followers, they don't have to agree with their leaders. I grew up in a small private secular martial arts school. I was told how to empty my mind in meditation and shown how to idolize a picture of a man on the wall. Even though I strongly disagreed with these teachings, I didn't abandon martial arts, nor did I accept the falsehood that Satan tried to plant. Instead, I learned and transformed the major concepts of martial arts into a tool for teaching Christian principles and values. I turned the concept of master from man to Christ and the concept of battle from physical to spiritual.

Being a follower is necessary to becoming a leader, but it doesn't automatically make you leader either. There are plenty of good martial artists that don't know how to teach and plenty of good Christians that don't know how to lead others to Christ. Leaders are street smart; they know how to reach people by getting into their socks and shoes. They have a way of relating to people and then filtering in the Good News about Christ. They don't write off sinners, they get in their lives and befriend them. Jesus was known as the friend of sinners and that was His secret to leadership. Jesus knew God extremely well, but He also knew the world.

As black belts, we need to know martial arts, but we also need to understand the world and how to fight in it. We don't win fights because we know how to kick, we win because we know what kind of kick to use, when to hold back or execute, what angle to set or not set, and how fast or slow to fire in any given situation, through lots of training. Being a Christian is quite the same; like Jesus, we need to learn how to be a friend in the world, but not of the world. We don't win people to Christ because we know the Bible really well, or because we can sin along with folks; we win because we know what scriptures to use, when to hold back or execute, what angle to set or not set, and how fast or slow to fire through lots of time with God in training.

PRINCIPLE	Good leaders are street smart; they know God but understand the world.
CODES	Proverbs 11:14
	2 Corinthians 2:14

1 Chronicles 1:10
Psalm 5:8

95. Mentoring

Mentoring is not leading; mentoring is teaching through a close, ongoing relationship between an older, mature individual and a young person. A mentor can take on many different roles with a "mentee." He/she can be a coach, a friend, a pal, a confidant, a listener, a guide, a partner, a supporter, a teacher, or a counselor. Although a mentor is a role model, a quality mentor does not expect a "mentee" to follow without reason. A quality mentor (1) gains the respect of a "mentee;" (2) is successful and admirable in an area of life where a "mentee" needs direction; (3) relates to a "mentee" in the area of needed direction; and (4) develops a close, ongoing relationship with him/her. All four of these ingredients must be present.

If I have succeeded and am admired for being a karate instructor, and all the qualities that go along with it, then I could probably be an effective mentor to a young girl who has low self-esteem and gets picked on at school. This is not only because I have high self-esteem and don't get picked on, but also because I used to be a girl with low-self esteem that got beat up by a gang after school every day. As you can see, no matter how successful and admired I am, I wouldn't be the best mentor for a fatherless boy who was in need of positive male direction in his life. I may be able to help him in some way, but I wouldn't be able to mentor him in the way that maybe a successful, fatherless, male karate instructor could mentor him if a relationship was established.

Jesus was a mentor to twelve ordinary men. He had positive, personal relationships with all of them, and through these relationships, the twelve ordinary men grew into the twelve disciples. They started out as blind followers, but over time became true "mentees." The men saw that Jesus experienced all of the things that they experienced. Although Jesus was God, He was fully human, too, and He knew all about hunger, thirst, fatigue, discomfort, pain, ridicule, betrayal, abuse, and suffering that we experience in our physical bodies. If you read the Bible, you will see that God's children have always been raised up through role modeling in relationships. Even God, Himself, was/is a mentor. He doesn't expect us to do anything that He has not already done, and He doesn't expect us to do anything outside of Him.

Paul said "Follow my example, as I follow the example of Christ" (1 Cor. 11:1, NIV). As Christian black belts, we are watched and we are pinpointed as mentors. People follow our example in everything! I've heard several parents even tell their children to follow my example; "Now if you want to be like Ms. Wendy, then you have to practice". Not only are we mentors in the martial arts, but also in the Christian way of life. Consequently, we must pay very close attention to what we do and say. Do you tell people to do as you do or to do as you say? Let us not forget, actions speak a lot louder than words. If we tell students to do anything that we don't do ourselves, then our credibility is diminished and our effectiveness fades away. When true mentoring relationships are established, however, they are incredibly powerful and transforming.

PRINCIPLE   Mentoring is the most powerful form of
             teaching that exists.

CODES	Titus 2:7-8
	John 13:15
	Matthew 4:19
	2 Thessalonians 3:9

96. Missionary

Christian black belt instructors are missionaries. Their mission is to spread the Good News about Jesus Christ in the modern-day world. They are good stewards of their God-given gifts, such as the ability to perform and teach martial arts with great skill. They use these gifts to do God's will on earth. To the Christian instructor, martial arts are also about training for spiritual warfare just as much as physical self-defense.

Being a missionary means having a mission, not traveling to far-away countries to teach and preach the Gospel. You can be a missionary in Africa or in a small town in Indiana. Missionary work is not where we serve; it's what we serve. People need to be reached all over the world. They need to be reached next door, down the street, and throughout your local community. Don't hesitate to step and reach out them. People need people and God.

Spreading the Good News requires more than standing on a street corner and preaching the Gospel or passing out Bibles to people who walk by. It requires finding common ground and interests with others. It means taking time to get to know and help people where they are, not where you'd like them to be. It means stepping out of your comfort zone by speaking and getting to know people you normally wouldn't associate with.

Martial arts aren't only for the rich and famous, and the Gospel isn't only for those who go to church. Let us reach out to our neighbors, to our friends, to our classmates, and to our colleagues and share with them what we know about Jesus, Sin, Salvation, and Eternal Life. People always ask me about Christian martial arts and it always opens a door for me to share. It's weird; it's different; not everyone agrees, but it works!

Christian martial arts are a creative and unique package that brings God's concepts to the street, to real life, when we aren't protected by walls of the church or parental guidance. We do not serve a passive God; we serve a God who fights and wins. Don't be afraid to learn how and teach others to fight. Fighting is the only way we can survive in a world where people are abused, abducted, raped, and murdered everyday. To fight is to win.

PRINCIPLE	Missionary work is defined by what we do, not where we go.
CODES	1 Corinthians 9:19
	1 Peter 4:10
	Mark 16:15

97. Protector

Christian black belts are protected under God because they have believed and received the ultimate safeguard that God sent to the world, Jesus Christ. As temples of God, they also protect God's children with martial arts skills and techniques and with spiritual laws and principles in the Bible. Christian black belts allow God to use them to protect souls. Without

God's ultimate safeguard in their lives (Jesus Christ), they are powerless.

God is a protector of His children
- The LORD shall preserve thee from all evil: he shall preserve thy soul. The LORD shall preserve thy going out and thy coming in from this time forth, and even for evermore (Ps. 121:7-8, KJV).

God strengthens His children
- But the Lord is faithful, who shall establish you, and keep you from evil (2 Thess. 3:3, KJV).

God empowers His children
- But now thus saith the LORD that created thee, O Jacob, and he that formed thee, O Israel, Fear not: for I have redeemed thee, I have called thee by thy name; thou art mine. When thou passest through the waters, I will be with thee; and through the rivers, they shall not overflow thee: when thou walkest through the fire, thou shalt not be burned; neither shall the flame kindle upon thee (Isa. 43:1-2, KJV).

The Name of the Lord is a source of protection
- The name of the LORD is a strong tower: the righteous runneth into it, and is safe (Prov. 18:10, KJV).

Listening is a source of protection
- But whoso hearkeneth unto me shall dwell safely, and shall be quiet from fear of evil (Prov. 1:33, KJV).

Obedience is a source of protection
- But if thou shalt indeed obey his voice, and do all that I speak; then I will be an enemy unto thine enemies,

and an adversary unto thine adversaries (Ex. 23:22, KJV).

Dwelling is a source of protection

- Because thou hast made the LORD, which is my refuge, even the most High, thy habitation; There shall no evil befall thee, neither shall any plague come nigh thy dwelling (Ps. 91:9-10, KJV).

PRINCIPLE	Jesus Christ is the source of our protection and our ability to protect.
CODES	See Above

98. Servant

The world believes that kings, queens, and other people in authority should be served. Even in martial arts, "good" students are taught to cater to and serve their instructors. However, the Bible teaches just the opposite; kings and queens should focus on serving, not being served. To become a better servant is to become more Christ-like. Christ Jesus was impeccably humble; "Who, being in very nature God, did not consider equality with God something to be grasped, but made himself nothing, taking the very nature of a servant, being made in human likeness" (Phil. 2:6-7, NIV).

Christ Jesus was a king who spent His entire lifetime serving others. He healed the sick, raised the dead, and performed all kinds of miracles for people. Christ served unto His death, and in His death, as the ultimate sacrifice for our sins. It is because of His service that we have a way to God the father.

Because of His service, we can know agape love and fellowship again with our creator through eternal life. Because of His service, God exalted Christ Jesus to the highest place in heaven and gave him a name above all names; every knee shall bow and every tongue shall confess that Jesus Christ is Lord of all (Phil. 2:9-11).

As martial artists of the Christian way, as students and followers of Jesus Christ, we train to serve. We serve by praying for people, teaching them, giving to them, and going out of our way to do things that help them. While tithing and giving gifts is important, we must also be willing to give our time and energy to people, too. True Christian black belts believe in and offer themselves to God's service by stepping up and protecting others when necessary. They don't sit back and watch evil happen and say "I wish things were different," they say "At your service…" and do God's will.

To serve is to combat evil, and while it's hard to understand, to fail to serve is to contribute to evil. Service is God's expression of love and hospitality to His children. When we serve, we allow God to give a big hug and kiss to someone who needs it, and we open a door for God to move in his/her life. Get right with God and serve Him. In doing so, you'll put out the devil's fires wherever you go and attract people to the Lord. Remember, as a military officer takes a pledge to serve his country, you take a pledge to serve the Lord Jesus Christ. In doing so, you are obliged to do His work and serve all God's children in the world.

PRINCIPLE   To serve is combat evil.

CODES   John 12:26
             Eph. 4:11-13

Matt. 20:28

99. Teacher (Sensei)

One of the requirements of Black Belts all over the world is to teach. Thus, a Black Belt must know the martial arts well. A Christian Black Belt must know the martial arts and God's Word well and be able to combine the major precepts of martial arts with the concepts of Christianity. Christian black belts are trained to use God's armor to knock down the Devil, expose his strategies, and bring people to Christ (2 Cor. 10:4-5).

Teaching is a learned art that begins as early as yellow belt. It's one thing to do martial arts and something all together different to teach it. Jesus was the master teacher because He reached all kinds of people in a way that no other human being has ever been able to do. He used stories and illustrations that made sense to people from all cultures and races (Mark 4:33). In a like manner, we use analogies from martial arts to teach people about Christ.

As a martial artist, you are studying self-defense while training your body for physical fitness. As a Christian, you are a student of the Holy Spirit (John 14:26) and follow the Bible as your primary text for life (Rom. 15:4). As a Christian martial artist, you are studying self-defense, while training your body, mind, and soul for spiritual fitness. As a Christian Black Belt, you are learning how to teach Christian martial arts to others and use your talents and abilities to glorify God. I am not a Master, and no matter how many ranks I obtain, I will never call myself a Master. I am a Teacher (a Sensei). I use my abilities and gifts to glorify my Lord and bring people to know and walk with my Master, Jesus Christ. Without Jesus I would have no strength, no abilities, and no gifts. I am what I am because of Him and you are what you are because of Him. Someday, when you reach a high rank in martial arts, do not be deceived into thinking you are a master.

PRINCIPLE	We can aspire to be good teachers, but there is only one Master and He is Jesus Christ.
CODES	Psalm 16:2
	Matthew 23:10
	John 14:26

100. The Code

The Samurai were highly respected and honorable warriors of Japan between the 9th and 12th centuries. They were very similar to the Knights of Medieval Europe in that they were high-class soldiers and followed a strict code for living. While the Knights of Medieval Europe adhered to the Code of Chivalry, the Samurai adhered to the Code of Bushido. Both codes emphasized courage, honor, loyalty, justice, right-eousness, altruism, integrity, politeness, purity, honesty, and benevolence. Bushido translates as "Way of the Warrior" and although the Code of Bushido was based on Japanese culture and religion, the Bible teaches many of the same ideals.

The difference between Bushido and the Bible is that the ideals of Bushido are achieved through the self and the ideals of the Bible are achieved through Christ. In fact, the disparity between many religions and Christianity is not the ideals that are taught, it's the WAY in which people try to achieve the ideals. When I lived and worked in Africa, my homestay family was Animist/Muslim. Every night my mother would write a prayer 300+ times on a small wooden board with ink made from tree bark, wash the board in water, and then drink the water that she used to wash the board. She believed that the more she wrote her prayer and consumed it, the more her god would be inclined to answer. If this sounds strange to you, then just think about your own culture and beliefs and how your actions might appear to an outsider; as a Christian, you symbolically eat the flesh and drink the blood of your God. Yikes!

You and I both know the meaning behind our Christian customs of communion, baptism, etc.; however, outsiders do not. So, how do you explain your religion and beliefs to others? For starters, Christianity is the only religion in the world that believes in a God who wants us to reach a set of ideals that we are incapable of reaching on our own. Thus, it's the only religion with a Savior. In the Old Testament, God gave us all sorts of ideals and our ancestors could not live up to them because of the iniquity that was passed from generation to generation after Adam and Eve allowed sin into their lives. As descendents of Adam and Eve, we all have sin in our lives and the only way we can come clean and approach God is to die to ourselves and allow Christ to live through us. It's Christ living through us who lives up to God's ideals, not us. However, through Christ's presence in our lives, we are sanctified.

In the New Testament, God told us to stop trying to live up to all His ideals, and instead, to get Christ. The plan was that we would do nothing to attain spiritual sanctification on our own but do everything to get Christ. God wants us to hunger and thirst for Christ, not strive for Biblical perfection. "Blessed are those who hunger and thirst for righteousness, for they will be filled" (Matt. 5:6, NIV). It's the path we walk, not the ideal we chase, which truly marks Christianity. Going to church more, praying more, sinning less, giving more, having more patience, being more loving, etc., are all ideals, the same as the Ten Commandments. All of these ideals are the result of having Christ in our lives. The goal is not to focus on obtaining the ideals; but rather, to focus on the path. Jesus said "I am the way and the truth and the life" (John 14:6, NIV), describing himself as the path, not the destination.

As Christian martial artists, our code is not Bushido, it's the Bible. Our way is not the Way of the Warrior, it's the Way of Christ; the Way of Christ will automatically make us Christian warriors. Folks, if you understand the following two points in the Bible, then you comprehend it all:

1. The path is Christ (John 14:6)

2. The ideal is Love (Matt. 22:37-40, Mark 12:30-31, and Luke 10:27)

So before you pray for more patience or love, stop and think. You really don't need more patience or love, you need more Christ. Remember, it's not about you, it's about Jesus. So, move over and let Him breathe, and His patience and love will shine through.

PRINCIPLE	Focus on the path, not the destination. Do everything you can to get Christ, not to become a good Christian.
CODES	Matthew 7:13
	Hebrews 12:13
	John 10:9

101. The Warrior

Every army in the world is called to defend the people of its nation when under threat or attack. In the same way, every Christian in the world is called to defend souls that are under threat or attack by evil and sin. Christians are members of an army under the Chief Commander Jesus Christ, who came to defeat Satan and save the lost children of God. Christian warriors are revolutionary people who actively rebel against the ways of this world and train in the principles, techniques, and strategies of God. They fight not only for God but also WITH God in all that they do.

As Christian martial artists, we are in essence training ourselves to serve among Jesus Christ's Special Forces of men and women. We train not only to defend the honor of God, with God, but also to defend people from mental, spiritual, and physical evil. Our focus is holistic and incorporates all aspects of life. If someone is physically safe but mentally in danger, then we do what we can to bring the mind of Christ to him/her through prayer, guidance, and counsel, by allowing God to work through us. Likewise, if one is mentally safe (with a mind of Christ) but physically in danger, then we use our martial arts techniques to bring safety, by again allowing God to work through us.

When you become a Christian black belt, you are accepting the position of "Warrior under Jesus Christ"; you are dedicating your life to defend the honor of God and protect people in the name of Jesus, with God at your side. You are committed to His service and His mission for mankind. You lay down your life to follow Him and His way and you pray for and guide others to do the same. You physically, mentally, and spiritually dispose of yourself to Jesus Christ and teach by example and through love according to the Holy Bible. Christ is your Commander in Chief, and God is your majesty and king.

David was the ideal role model of a Christian warrior. He had a heart to defend the honor of God and protect his people against the Philistines. He also had the determination and courage to do it by himself, with God, if that is what it took. David was confident in his God-given abilities and his faith was strong. He didn't depend on fancy weapons and armor to win, but on the Lord to fight with him in strength and power. A simple sling shot, five stones, and the name of Lord is all David needed to win this fight. David knew who he was and what he stood for. There was no doubt in his mind that this battle was the Lord's and the Lord would prevail through him, so he was not intimidated or afraid.

Goliath tried to intimidate David just before the big fight, but David didn't allow it and shouted back to him, "You come to me with sword, spear, and javelin, but I come to you in the name of the LORD Almighty—the God of the armies of Israel, whom you have defied. Today the LORD will conquer you, and I will kill you and cut off your head. And then I will give the dead bodies of your men to the birds and wild

animals, and the whole world will know that there is a God in Israel! And everyone will know that the LORD does not need weapons to rescue his people. It's his battle, not ours. The LORD will give you to us!" (1 Sam. 17:45-47, NLT).

PRINCIPLE	A Christian warrior depends on and confides in God to win battles.
CODES	Exodus 15:3

Judges 6:12
Psalm 33:16
Jeremiah 20:11
Psalm 91:4

Index

ATTENTION INSTRUCTORS!

Order *Martial Arts: The Christian Way* for your school now!

Order *Christian Martial Arts 101* for you or your students!

Agapy Publishing offers a 40%-50% discount off their retail prices to martial arts programs, schools, ministries, churches, outreach groups, and teams that purchase the same book in quantities of 6 or more. Send an email to info@agapy.com for information and details. Also, visit http://www.agapy.com for an updated list of products.

SPECIAL COUPON

Order 25 copies of *Christian Martial Arts 101* (Retail Value of $15.95 each) for $200, 50% off! plus $20 shipping. In addition to this already fabulous offer, get a free copy of *Martial Arts: The Christian Way* (a retail value of $12.95).

OR

Order 25 copies of *Martial Arts: The Christian Way* (Retail Value of $12.95 each) for $150, 55% off! plus $20 shipping.

Place your order today! www.agapy.com/cma/orderform.html

Valid for one order per customer, per lifetime.
Coupon Code: CMA101InstructorPromo

Visit the *Christian Martial Arts Network* for information and about Christian martial arts. It hosts a large, international directory of associations and schools that support and teach Christian martial arts. http://www.agapy.com/cma

CPSIA information can be obtained
at www.ICGtesting.com
Printed in the USA
LVOW03s1219040517
533196LV00001B/112/P